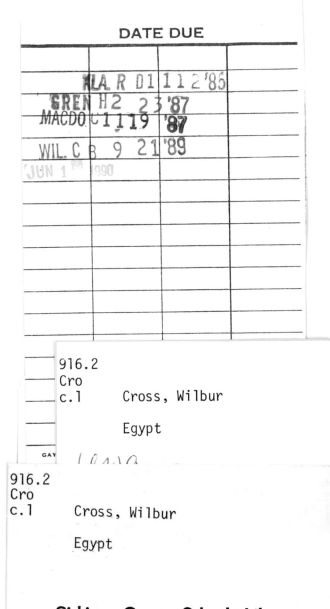

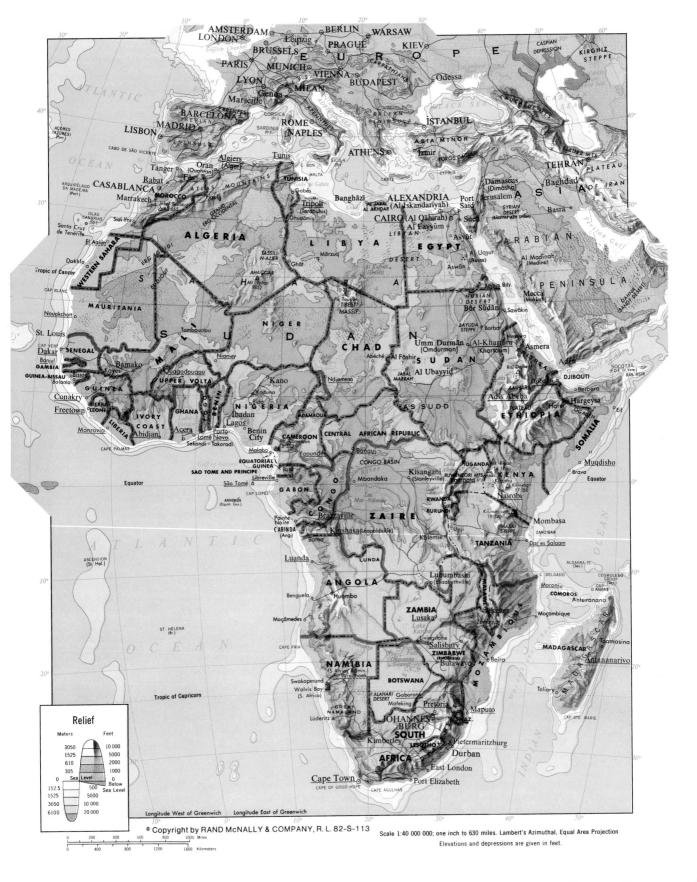

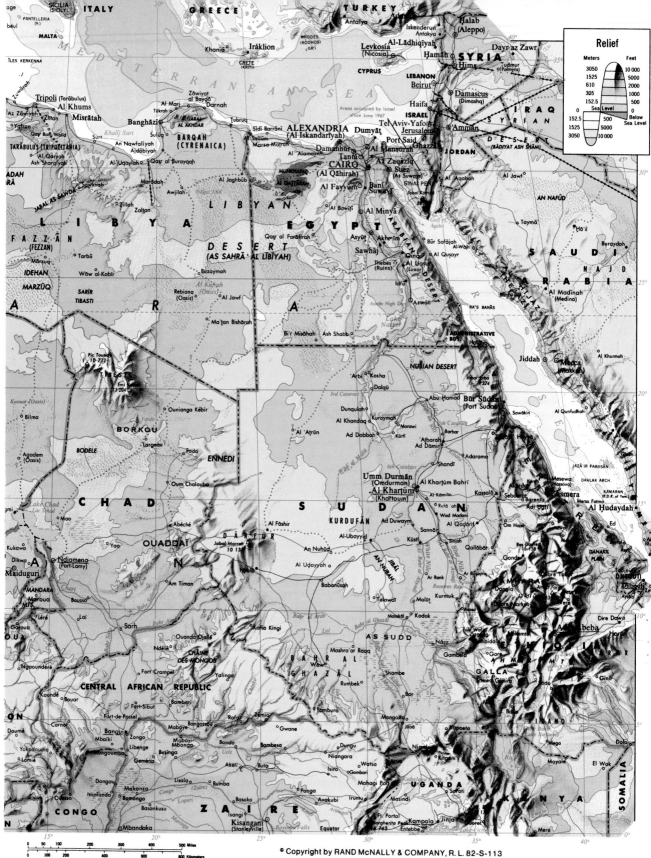

*Enchantment of the World*

# EGYPT

*By Wilbur Cross*

**Consultant:** Osama Sadek, Egyptian Journalist

**Consultant for Social Studies:** Donald W. Nylin, Ph. D., Assistant
Superintendent for Instruction, Aurora West Public Schools, Aurora, Illinois

**Consultant for Reading:** Robert L. Hillerich, Ph.D., Bowling Green State
University, Bowling Green, Ohio

 CHILDRENS PRESS, CHICAGO

*Street in the Khan el Khalili bazaar, Cairo*

**Picture Acknowledgments:**
**Colour Library International** — 4, 11, 21, 29, 31, 44, 47, 59, 61 (2 photos), 69, 70 (left), 72, 82, 86, 91, 94, 101, 103, 105, 109 (right top and bottom), 112
**Historical Picture Services** — 38, 42 (2 photos), 46 (2 photos), 53, 57
**Melaine Ristich** — 5, 6, 17, 19, 26, 33, 34, 55, 67 (top), 75 (lower left), 79, 92 (2 photos), 98
**United Press International, Inc.** — 62 (2 photos), 64 (2 photos), 107
**Root Resources:**   © P.L. Ames — 9 (top), 18, 73, 74 (top);
© J. C. Ringenoldus — 12 (bottom);
© Roger J. Naser — 12 (top), 23, 67 (bottom), 85
**Harry and Pat Michalski** — 9 (bottom), 75 (top, bottom right), 76, 78, 109 (left, top and bottom), 110
**Chandler Forman** — 10, 70 (right), 74 (bottom)
**The Metropolitan Museum of Art** — 80 (bottom), 96, 97
Rogers Fund, 1912 — 25 (left)
Rogers Fund, 1935 — 25 (right)
Museum Excavations and Rogers Fund, 1930 — 28
Museum Excavations (1913-1914) and Rogers Fund, 1914 — 30
Gift of Edward S. Harkness, 1917 — 36
Gift of Theodore M. Davis, 1909 — 37 (top)
Contribution from Henry Walters and the Rogers Fund, 1916 — 37 (bottom)
The Carnarvon Collection, Gift of Edward S. Harkness, 1926 — 39
Rogers Fund, 1909 — 50 (left)
Rogers Fund, 1930 — 50 (right)
Rogers Fund, 1950 — 58
Purchase 1968, Lila Acheson Wallace Fund, Inc. — 80 (top)

Library of Congress Cataloging in Publication Data

Cross, Wilbur.
    Egypt.

    (Enchantment of the world)
    Includes index.
    Summary: Discusses the history, physical characteristics, economy, and culture of the land which has been called the gift of the Nile.
    1. Egypt — Juvenile literature. [1. Egypt]
I. Title. II. Series.
DT49.C76   1982        962        82-9465
ISBN 0-516-02762-X              AACR2

*Arab women doing laundry at the village pump*

TABLE OF CONTENTS

Chapter 1:   *Egypt: Land of the Sun* (An Introduction). . . . . 7

Chapter 2:   *The Living Map* (Geography). . . . . 15

Chapter 3:   *The Rich Tapestry of History* (Ancient Egypt to Modern-day Republic). . . . . 24

Chapter 4:   *The Sprouting Cities and Towns* (Life in Modern Egypt). . . . . 65

Chapter 5:   *Seeds of the Economy* (Industry and Agriculture). . . . . 81

Chapter 6:   *Cultural Enhancements* (The Arts and Education). . . . . 95

Chapter 7:   *The Faces of a Nation* (People and Their Customs). . . . . 106

*Minifacts at a Glance.* . . . . 116

*Index.* . . . . 125

*Nomads still travel across Egypt's deserts living very much as their ancestors did hundreds of years ago.*

# Chapter 1

# EGYPT:

## LAND OF THE SUN

Throughout their long and unusual history, the people of Egypt have always worshiped the sun as a god. It is easy to see why, in a land where there are seldom any clouds and where there is less rainfall in an entire year than might fall in your own backyard on a single stormy afternoon.

The sun dictates many things in Egypt: the types of clothing worn; the design of homes and public buildings; the kinds of crops grown; the daily round of activities. It is perfectly natural then that this celestial body should have been looked upon as a god in ancient times, and right down through thousands of years. Even the night was accounted for without in any way diminishing the role of the sun god. The people observed that the sun rose in the East and set in the West. So it was easy to imagine that the fiery god was riding in a boat from one side of the sky to the other and then going down through the nether, or underworld, regions until morning.

# SUNLIT LAND

The geography of Egypt is so unique that it is not matched even by those nations that share its climate and general location along the southern shores of the Mediterranean. About 90 percent of the country is desert.

The sun beats down fiercely, turning the desert sands into a dusty griddle. Curiously enough, when night falls the desert becomes bitterly cold. There is no such thing as a "mild" time of day except perhaps for brief spells at dusk and at dawn.

In the large cities like Alexandria and Port Said on the coast to the north, and Cairo in the northern delta region, the dry climate is more hospitable. It is less influenced by the harsh desert.

The average temperatures in Alexandria during the day range from about 50° F. (10° Celsius) in the winter to the mid-80s (about 30° Celsius) in the middle of summer. Cairo is much the same, though the temperature can drop to as low as 45° F. (7.2° Celsius) in the winter and rise to as high as 95° F. (35° Celsius) in the summer. Unlike Alexandria, Cairo does not have the waters of the Mediterranean to soften its climate.

In Luxor and Aswan, much farther south and nearer the equator, the temperatures are about thirty degrees higher.

Foreigners who visit Egypt are struck by two facts. First, since there are no clouds or mists, the colors (whether natural or man-made) are all sharp and well-defined, day after day. Second, and for the same reason, the colors never change.

The unchanging climate in Egypt was in some ways a boon to ancient Egyptians. Their architects and priests invented many astronomical instruments. They used them to observe the

The Bedouin tent (above) is typical of the shelter used by nomadic desert dwellers.
But in urban areas, such as Cairo (below), high-rise apartments and hotels are commonplace.

*The Pyramid of Giza (Al Jīzah) stands not far from the modern capital of Egypt, Cairo. More than two million stone blocks were used to build this gigantic structure.*

changing positions of heavenly bodies. The Great Pyramid of Giza was, in a sense, an astronomical instrument. Quite recently, scientists made an astonishing discovery. They found that, by looking through what appeared to be ventilation shafts towards the sky, they could identify specific constellations of stars and accurately determine their movements through the heavens over a given period of time.

Why was such celestial movement of any value to the ancient Egyptians? For one thing, their observations helped them to devise an accurate calendar. They could also anticipate changes in

*Temple at Karnak*

the seasons. These were meaningful in the planting of crops or the planning of sea voyages and overland trips by caravan. Based on their observations they established the beginning of the Egyptian year as the exact moment when Sirius (known as the "Dog Star") rose in a certain position at dawn. This event was of special significance in the life of an agricultural people for it marked the date when the Nile River would begin flooding.

The vast temple of Amon-Ra, the sun god, at Karnak serves this astronomical purpose, too. It was so designed that it would record the arrival of the winter solstice. At dawn on this day the rays of the sun shine exactly on the temple altar.

11

Cairo (above) is built on the banks of the Nile River.
In the nearby countryside (below) both ancient and modern irrigation
systems are used to bring water to the crops.

The river Nile is also influenced by the sun. Each spring, the sun melts the snows in the high mountain ranges of East Africa where the Nile originates in its two sources, the White Nile and the Blue Nile. As the snow melts, the streams become gorged with water. By the time they reach upper Egypt they represent a tremendous force. Today, the waters are controlled by dams, canals, water gates, and other works, but in ancient times they simply flooded the land. When the flood waters receded, the fields were enriched with layers of new soil—all thanks to the power of the sun.

The early Egyptians explained spiritual life, as well as earthly life, in terms of what they could *see.* The high cliffs surrounding some of the valleys were pillars that supported the heavens. The river was the source of transportation to the afterworld. The deserts were the boundaries beyond which there was no human life. Shining above this limited world, the sun was the source of life, synonymous with fertility. As a god, the sun could have many forms. He could appear as a hawk, a beetle, or a bull. Sometimes he might take the form of an old man or a young stranger.

No matter where or in what image the sun god appeared, he was all-seeing. People who defied customs or were lazy would quickly be found out. But those who paid homage to these gods and did the work assigned to them could expect a rewarding life in the afterworld.

All these facts reveal why Egypt has been and still is called the Land of the Sun.

Cairo

Nile River

Lake Nasser

# Chapter 2

# THE LIVING MAP

## THE TREE OF NOURISHMENT

From high in a spacecraft the Arab Republic of Egypt is a remarkable sight. It resembles a kind of gigantic brown poster, bordered on two sides by blue water. From top to bottom, somewhat off center, is what looks like a scrawny green tree, with a crooked trunk, and a fan of branches at the top.

On a conventional map, Egypt is squarish in shape, bordered on the north by the Mediterranean, on the east by the Red Sea, and cut from north to south by 900 miles (1,448 kilometers) of the longest river in the world, the mighty Nile. Writing about Egypt in the fifth century B.C., the Greek historian Herodotus said the country was "the gift of the river." In his opinion, Egypt owed its very existence to the Nile, as the only real source of water and nourishment in an otherwise barren terrain.

Nowhere else, in history or geography, has a nation been so dominated by a single natural feature. It is a rather dramatic fact that the Nile originates more than three thousand miles (4,827 kilometers) from the border of Egypt in a remote headstream, the Luvironza River, in the heart of Africa.

The Nile enters Egypt at the northern border of the Sudan. This is its broadest point, where long, man-made Lake Nasser was formed by the Aswan High Dam after its completion in 1971. From here the Nile flows steadily northward, with a few zigs and zags, finally branching out into numerous distributaries that form the fan-shaped delta as they flow into the Mediterranean. The enormity of the water flow is shown by the fact that the Nile drains an area of some 1.1 million square miles (2,849,000 square kilometers) or about one tenth of the entire African continent.

## THE RIBBONS OF GREEN

Flowing through the heart of some of the greatest deserts in the world, the Nile is like a gigantic leaking hose. Water seeps out along its entire length. The water and silt, carried from the African highlands, form the ribbon of fertile soil which has produced the crops that make it continually green. In ancient times and right up until this century, however, crops regularly were ruined by floods that were easy to predict but difficult to control.

The floodplain, or ribbon, is very narrow, only 2 to 5 miles (3.2 to 8 kilometers) wide for most of its route from Aswan 550 miles (885 kilometers) north to Cairo. But at Cairo, the capital, the fertile ribbon broadens into a valley some 15 miles (24 kilometers) across, in which crops can be grown, particularly wheat, corn, cotton, and rice.

The Aswan Dam, completed in 1902 and twice improved; the Aswan High Dam; and a modern network of irrigation ditches, pipelines, canals, and holding basins all have contributed to a much more efficient system than in the past. They have created a wider and greener ribbon than ever was conceived of in the days of the pharaohs.

*Village not far from the modern city of Cairo*

## THE DELTA FAN

North of Cairo lies a great fan-shaped delta, some 100 miles (161 kilometers) long and about 120 miles (193 kilometers) at its widest point. Two main distributaries, the Rosetta River on the west and the Damietta River on the east, carry the waters of the Nile or what remains after irrigation for the final 150 miles (241 kilometers) to the sea. They in turn are broken into smaller distributaries forming the "webs" of the fan.

It is here, in the great Nile Delta, that is found a good 60 percent of the tillable soil in the entire country. Ironically, in a land that is 95 percent desert, the delta has large areas of shallow lakes and swamps that are unfit for cultivation.

The impact of geography on human settlement and the course of history is clearly illustrated in Egypt. The people settle along the course of the Nile.

*Acacia grove in the Qattara Depression*

## THE OCEANS OF SAND

At least 95 percent of the republic of Egypt is desert and wasteland. The two greatest masses, part of the Sahara Desert system, are the Western Desert and the Eastern Desert. They are separated from each other by the Nile River. The Western Desert is an extension of the Libyan Desert. The Eastern Desert is sometimes referred to as the Arabian Desert. In the southeast, Egypt is touched by the Nubian Desert, lying mainly in the Sudan.

Only about 15 percent of these deserts have sand dunes of the type commonly shown in motion pictures. The deserts of Egypt are made up of rock outcroppings, coarse gravel, and in some places barren hills and mountains. The Qattara Depression, a basin in northwestern Egypt, covers 7,000 square miles (18,130 square kilometers). It is the lowest point in Africa, sinking to 436 feet (133 meters) below sea level at its deepest position.

The Sahara Desert system has one of the harshest climates in the world. The desert is a place with intense heat and glaring sun. The region also is subject to strong winds blowing incessantly from the northeast. Dry periods can last for years. Daytime

*Scene along the road to Faiyum (Al Fayyum)*

temperatures can hover around 120° F. (49° Celsius), yet drop to 40° F. (4.4° Celsius) at night, or to freezing during the period from December to February.

Sparse vegetation can be found in those parts of the desert that do not consist of shifting sands and dunes. In recent years, scientists have found that even these wastelands support unusual colonies of animal and insect life.

Egypt has five important oases, all in the Western Desert: Farafirah, Bahriyah, Dakhilah, Kharijah, and Siwah. They are green islands in the oceans of sand, complete with palm trees and other vegetation, springs of fresh water, and small populations. Many of the inhabitants are nomadic.

19

## THE BORDERING SEAS

Although the Red Sea forms the longest portion of the eastern border of Egypt, there are few towns on the coast and no major ports. Access to the sea is denied by the wall of forbidding mountains that characterize most of the Eastern Desert.

At the northern end of the Red Sea lies the narrow Gulf of Suez. This became an important waterway for Egypt and other Mediterranean nations when the Suez Canal opened in 1869.

The desirability of a waterway between the Mediterranean and the Red seas goes back to ancient times. Ancient records show that canals were built to connect existing lakes and make possible a better trade route and travel at least part of the way by boat.

The Red Sea was named for the reddish algae that appear in its very warm waters during part of the year.

The Mediterranean Sea is the world's largest inland sea. It takes its name from the Latin for "in the midst of lands." It has always been of prime importance to Egypt, especially to the Nile Delta region that bulges into it. From Cairo inland at the start of the delta to the large seaports of Alexandria and Port Said, the Mediterranean has served Egypt, for better and worse, down through the ages. Without its waters, the country would have had little commerce or communication with the outside world.

For modern Egypt, seeking to use its technology to produce oil, chemicals, and metals for export, the Mediterranean is a front door to world trade.

*Cargoes are loaded and unloaded at Port Said on the Mediterranean Sea.*

# TOPOGRAPHICAL FEATURES
# ENHANCED BY HUMAN SKILLS

In Egypt technology has transformed many geographical
negatives into historical positives. Two such transformations were
milestones:

(1) The opening of the Suez Canal.

(2) The completion of the Aswan High Dam in 1971,
complementing the earlier (1902) Aswan Dam, opened some two
million acres (809,400 hectares) of desert land to cultivation, and
multiplied energy power tenfold.

Technology and improved planning have added to the
efficiency of the irrigation system along the Nile. They have also
eliminated or reduced the loss of crops through flooding or
drought, thus bringing the ecology of the region into balance.

Egypt's future economy is currently focused on two
geographical regions. These are the Gulf of Suez and the Sinai
Peninsula. The geology of both locations is such that Egypt can
hope to produce crude oil, both offshore and on land, in the near
future.

Such accomplishments would make the Suez Canal connecting
the Red Sea and the Mediterranean vitally significant to Egypt's
future.

Much of the Sinai was lost to Egypt when it was occupied by
Israel during the Six-Day War in 1967. But it was regained in 1982
under the terms of a 1979 peace treaty between the two countries.
Today the region's border on the east is marked by heavy concrete
blocks every kilometer from the northernmost town, Rafah, on the
Mediterranean, to Taba, on the Gulf of Aqaba.

*Panoramic view of Cairo*

## LAND OF THE SUN

Egypt's rainfall is slight, ranging from about ten inches (254 millimeters) annually along the Mediterranean to perhaps one inch (25 millimeters) in Cairo. The climate is divided into only two seasons: winter, from December through March, and summer, the rest of the year. Temperatures during the winter range from a low 50° F. (10° Celsius) to a high 70° F. (21° Celsius). Summers are hot, ranging from 80° F. (27° Celsius) to over 100° F. (38° Celsius). Yet the changes are gradual from one month to the next. Egypt does not have the sudden temperature changes typical of American and European cities.

The desert is quite the opposite, often with enormous daily variations of temperatures, very hot in the day and cold at night. This happens because there is absolutely no humidity to maintain the even balance found in the cultivated regions.

The Mediterranean areas enjoy cooling sea breezes. During the summer the wind blows from the north right up the Nile valley, keeping communities along the river cooler. But the wind most associated with Egypt is, unfortunately, the khamsin. This wind creates sandstorms in the desert, and also brings dust and grit to towns and cities in its path. It may continue off and on for as long as eight weeks in March, April, and May.

# Chapter 3

# *THE RICH TAPESTRY*
# *OF HISTORY*

---

Our knowledge of the past is constantly being pieced together like the parts of an enormous jigsaw puzzle. Many of the pieces are tiny and faded. These tell of isolated civilizations that emerged, thrived, declined, and vanished in several centuries or less. Fortunately, many of the pieces are large. They provide graphic insights into the past. The greatest contribution of all comes from the historical records of Egypt. No other country in the world goes back so far into the past, starting four thousand years before the birth of Christ.

Egypt's history spans almost six thousand years. Historical records have been found on stone tablets, in tombs laden with objects from the past, and in writings on papyrus, one of the earliest forms of paper. Fortunately, these ancient records have been well preserved by the hot, dry climate.

There was another Egypt, going back perhaps thirteen thousand years. This was when wandering tribes settled along the Nile and began to cultivate the land. In the Stone Age prehistoric people began settling in parts of the Nile valley. The soil was rich and water plentiful. In the later Neolithic period their descendants moved south to what was to be called Upper Egypt.

*This vessel was made more than four thousand years ago. The designs used mark this as an advanced civilization.*

*The scarab was crafted during the reign of Amenhotep III, who ruled about 1580 B.C. Such ornaments were used as a symbol of good fortune. It was also a symbol of resurrection.*

There were three distinct cultures that formed during this early period: the Badarian, in the district of Badari; Amratian, with its center at a village called Naqada; and Gerzean, near the Second Cataract of the Nile. Burying grounds have been found. These tell us that the people of this civilization had discovered copper and were able to fashion it into very simple tools and ornaments. Pottery was well made and sometimes painted with symbols and subjects that give further clues to the people's interests. Some of these early Egyptians discovered how to make bricks by shaping mud from the banks of the Nile and drying it in the sun.

This early period has been named Predynastic (coming before the periods that later were to be known as dynasties). By the end of this period, the country became divided into two parts. Upper

*View of the landscape where the desert and irrigated land meet.*
*Vast irrigation projects have turned barren deserts into farmland.*

Egypt had its capital at Hierakonpolis. Lower Egypt, which
covered the area of the Nile Delta, close to the Mediterranean Sea,
had its capital at Buto.

## THE GIFT OF THE NILE

When the Greek historian Herodotus referred to Egypt as "the
gift of the river" he meant, of course, that the country owed its
very existence and later development to the Nile River. This was
true in those earliest times, as can be seen in the locations of all of
the remains from the Stone Age and the Neolithic period. There
are a number of puzzles in the picture, however, that never have
been solved. One of the greatest concerns the nature of the land
itself. Historians now are certain that many thousands of years
ago the lands on both sides of the Nile—which today are vast
deserts—were green. The land had forests and animals. No one
knows what enormous natural event occurred that made deserts
out of once fertile soil.

Why did rainfall cease almost entirely? We may never know. But historians do feel that this change caused people to move gradually over a span of thousands of years to the river valleys.

Around the year 3200 B.C., the first real ruler of Egypt took over. This man, whom we call Menes, began as king of Upper Egypt (known as the White Kingdom because the king wore a white crown, symbol of a land that was largely white in color, except for the strip of green along the Nile). Menes was a strong leader. He pushed his people into acquiring more and more land along the river as it flowed downstream (or northward) toward the Mediterranean.

It was inevitable that Menes eventually would take over Lower Egypt (known as the Red Kingdom because of the color of the Nile mud). There is no record of war, yet not long after the beginning of his reign Menes was wearing a combination white-and-red crown, symbol of the "Kingdom of the Two Lands."

Thus was founded the First Dynasty. It continued for a little more than two hundred years and had its capital at the city of Memphis. For the first time in its history, Egypt was a single nation, largely as it is today in geographical terms, dependent upon the Nile for its lifeblood.

Information about the people of the First Dynasty and the reign of Menes is abundant. Historians know about life as it was in and around the old city of Memphis, located only 20 miles (32 kilometers) from the site where Cairo later would be built.

## THE OLD KINGDOM

The dynasty of Menes was the beginning of what is now referred to as the Old Kingdom or the Old Empire. During the 950

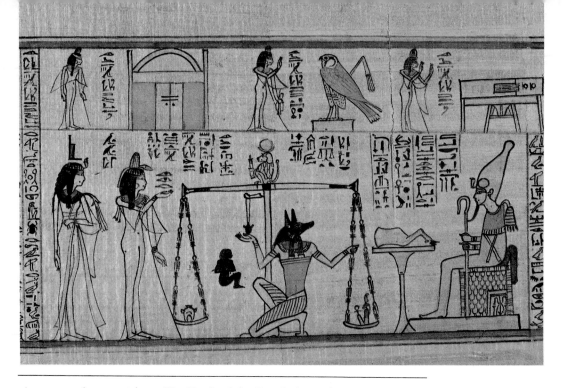

*A papyrus document from* The Book of the Dead *shows the weighing of the human heart. It was discovered in the tomb of a Queen Meryet-amun and dates from about 1025 B.C.*

years of this era, the Egyptians accomplished some remarkable feats. These include the building of the great Pyramids, the invention of paper, and the method of mummifying the dead.

With achievements such as these, plus methods of irrigating desert lands and producing crops, the Egyptians set what was the most remarkable record of all—their civilization lasted almost without interruption for some thirty centuries.

One of the reasons we know so much about the Egyptian dynasties is that the people learned how to take papyrus reeds, pound them into fibrous pulp, and eventually produce sheets of white, smooth paper. Then they perfected an early system of writing called hieroglyphics that consisted of tiny pictures and symbols. It was first used by the priests to show the acts of the various gods and to express religious beliefs. Gradually, record keeping became important for all aspects of daily life.

*Statue of Horus*

A related achievement was the development of a calendar not unlike the one in use today. Each year had 360 days, plus a period of five sacred feast days at the end. Many of the other days on the calendar also represented periods of religious significance. In fact, there was no aspect of record keeping or daily life that somehow was not tied in with religion and the gods.

The king himself, called the pharaoh, was considered a god. He was referred to as "the son of Ra" or "Horus on earth," and was thought to be related to the heavenly god everyone worshiped. These Egyptians were motivated by the presence of this living god. They believed that by working hard and doing good works that the pharaoh himself could observe, they would assure themselves a place in the afterlife.

*Statue of Twelfth Dynasty king wearing the red crown of northern or Lower Egypt*

Much of what we know about the pharaohs and the people can be traced to the Third to Sixth Dynasties when great architectural wonders were created. The period, often referred to as a classic era never surpassed in the history of ancient Egypt, lasted for about five hundred years. It all started with a farsighted king named Zoser. He felt the time had come for the nation to start building structures so solid and so enormous that they would survive forever as evidence that Egypt was the greatest kingdom on earth.

The king summoned Imhotep, a member of his court, who already had demonstrated great skill at designing and constructing buildings. He had completed an aboveground tomb of a type referred to today as a mastaba. It was oblong in shape, with sloping sides, some 20 or 30 feet  (6.1 to 9.1 meters) in

*The Step Pyramid of Zoser at Sakkara was built during the Third Dynasty.*

height, and was typical of others built in Egypt and elsewhere. But Imhotep had an imaginative idea. Why not build an enormous mastaba tomb, squarish at the base, rather than oblong, and on top of that a whole series of similar structures, each one slightly smaller than the one beneath it?

He demonstrated his design with a model made of clay and immediately won the pharaoh's approval. The result was a famous monument, the Step Pyramid, which rose in six steps (not all exactly equal) to a height of some 200 feet (61 meters). Deep inside this mighty structure was a burial shaft and tomb chamber destined for use by the king in his afterlife. As the building progressed, other chambers were added to accommodate members of the royal family and store clothing, equipment, food, and other items needed by royalty after leaving life on earth.

This first historic pyramid was set within a magnificent rectangular court that had fine statues and pillars carved to resemble bundles of papyrus stalks. It was the model for others, including the three Pyramids of Giza. But the greatest of all, one of the Seven Wonders of the Ancient World, was the Great Pyramid of Cheops, the pharaoh who ruled during the Fourth Dynasty. Built around 2650 B.C., the Pyramid of Cheops (sometimes called Khufu) was a remarkable engineering achievement. The base alone, running more than 750 feet (229 meters) along each of the four sides, covered an area of some 13 acres (5.3 hectares). The pointed top rose at least 480 feet (146 meters) above the ground and may at one time have been crowned with some form of superstructure. Engineers have estimated that as many as 2.3 million blocks of stone were used for the pyramid itself, many of them weighing 15 tons (14 metric tonnes) and none less than three tons (2.7 metric tonnes).

Even more remarkable than the massive size was the accuracy of construction. A surveyor using modern instruments found that structural angles were off by less than one tenth of a degree. Furthermore, the huge blocks had been cut so carefully that the cracks between them are never wider than one fiftieth of an inch—barely wide enough to insert a razor blade!

The interior of the Great Pyramid of Cheops is equally impressive. It has endless corridors and shafts leading to a great number of subterranean chambers, one of which is 153 feet (47 meters) long and 28 feet (8.5 meters) high.

The designers and builders of the Pyramids had to be very clever. They built false doors, concealed entrances, and special locks, so that would-be thieves could not find certain corridors or the chambers housing the possessions of the departed pharaohs.

*Entrance to the Great Pyramid of Cheops. Concealed vaults and countless passages are found inside this remarkable tomb, which was built without the use of iron tools. It originally was sheathed in polished marble.*

*Statues of Ramses II, Amon of Thebes, Ptah of Memphis, and Re-Harakhty of Heliopolis found at Abu Simbel. On October 20 and February 20 these statues are lit by the rays of the sun shining into the temple. The Egyptians used their knowledge of astronomy to make these massive monuments giant scientific instruments.*

## THE FIRST INTERMEDIATE PERIOD

By the time of the Sixth Dynasty, starting in 2420 B.C., the great period of building was already on the decline. Pepi II, who became pharaoh at the age of six and reigned for the incredible span of ninety years, actually was a weak leader.

Consequently, the power of the throne diminished. This era was marked by the splitting of the kingdom into feudal zones. Each zone was governed by a ruler who was likely to be at odds with neighboring rulers and even with the pharaoh himself. The internal strife was so great that this First Intermediate Period later was know as the Period of Troubles.

For the first time in eight hundred years, the people began to wonder whether the pharaoh really was a god, since he seemed unable to unite the kingdom and put an end to the quarrels of the nobles. Even worse, many of the rulers of the feudal zones began imposing heavy taxes. In some cases, the people were oppressed in other ways, and were forced to labor long hours with little reward. The seat of power—the capital of the country—shifted from Memphis to Heracleopolis, a further sign that the government was weak.

This troubled period did not last long. Fortunately, the Twelfth Dynasty, known as the Middle Kingdom, saw the return of unity and prosperity under a number of pharaohs, among them Amenemhet I, II, III, and IV, and Sesostris I, II, and III. They were strong leaders and unified the people. They also started and maintained a growing trade with other Mediterranean countries, particularly Crete, Greece, Syria, and Palestine. Ships and caravans carried Egyptian materials and products to trade for wood, pottery, perfumes, olives, tin, and other metals.

The Egyptians generally were peaceful in their relationships with other neighbors. But they did invade other countries at this time. After conquering most of the African land to the south, the Egyptians built fortresses to protect their trade routes. These routes ran south into Punt (now Somaliland) on the Red Sea, where Egyptian traders obtained rich perfumes and other products. Only in recent times have the locations of several such fortresses been found through infrared aerial photography. Infrared photos can detect the scars on the landscape, even though the structures fell apart or were destroyed more than three thousand years ago.

The Middle Kingdom has been called Egypt's "second period of greatness" because of the accomplishments attained over a period of a little more than two hundred years. Internally, extensive irrigation programs were carried out, making better use of the

*This glazed painted figure of a hippopotamus was made during the Twelfth Dynasty.*

waters of the Nile and supplying the people with varied and plentiful crops. Crafts of all kinds were encouraged. This dynasty is noted for its jewelry, fine pottery, statuary, and other art forms. Literature reached new heights, as did language and music. Many reforms were made, making life pleasanter and more rewarding for the common people.

Ceramic pottery (above) discovered in the Valley of the Kings,
is believed to be an example of art from the Seventeenth Dynasty.
Leopard-head girdle and ankle jewelry (below) were crafted
during the Twelfth Dynasty.

*King Sesostris III*

Egypt now was an important nation in international trade. Its trade moved along land routes and in ships across the Mediterranean and up and down the Red Sea. By this time, the most important city was Thebes. Thebes was located much farther up the Nile than either Memphis or Heracleopolis. It was closer to Nubia and to the major part of the Red Sea, both of which were important to the Egyptian economy. Nevertheless, the area to the north where the earlier capitals had been established remained important, particularly the Faiyum. This fertile pocket of land near the Pyramids was the source of many major crops and was a strong factor in Egypt's new prosperity.

As the country grew in administrative and economic strength, the rulers during the Twelfth Dynasty felt an urge to expand the borders, as well as the trade routes. Thus the Egyptians invaded Syria for the first time, under Sesostris III, who served as his own

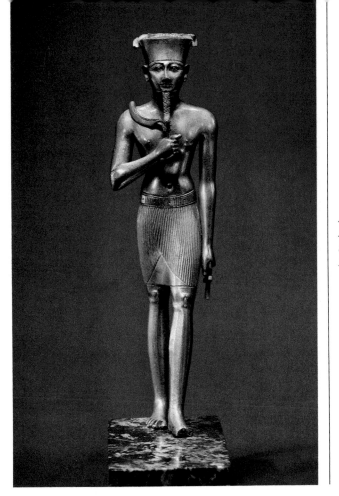

*A gold statue of Amon found near the Great Temple of Amon at Karnak*

first general in the field. Egypt was now an international power in the Mediterranean, as well as along some 1,000 miles (1,609 kilometers) of the Nile River.

Another development at the time was religious in nature. A god named Amon became important. Although Amon had been worshiped as an obscure lesser deity in Thebes, he now was revered as the god who protected Egyptian soldiers and traders as they traveled to other lands. He was honored each year when the Nile reached flood stage and spread its waters over the fields and deserts. The most massive temple in history, stretching for one quarter of a mile (.4 kilometers) would one day be built at Karnak in honor of Amon-Ra, king of the gods.

# SECOND INTERMEDIATE PERIOD
# AND START OF THE NEW KINGDOM

The Middle Kingdom eventually declined, as had earlier dynasties, because of internal strife and a growing lack of unity among the people.

As the power of the pharaohs weakened, Egypt became open to invasion. The Thirteenth through the Seventeenth Dynasties saw a two-hundred-year period of instability, known as the Second Intermediate Period. The country actually slipped back to the Predynastic era when it had been split into Upper and Lower Egypt. The squabbling among district leaders and the weakness of the central government made Egypt an easy target.

Consequently, the Hyksos, members of a brutal Asian tribe, invaded northern Egypt. The Hyksos (known also as the Shepherd Kings) crossed the desert, probably from Palestine. Their objective was to capture small towns, one after another, which they could easily hold in subjugation, living off the bounty of the land and the products of the artisans.

At first the Egyptians were unable to resist. The Hyksos had developed superior weapons of war, particularly the horse-drawn chariot, for which Egyptian foot soldiers were no match. Ironically, however, as the Hyksos settled in, learned Egyptian ways, and became less alert, they also became weaker. Gradually the Egyptians regained their military strength and overcame the enemy in their midst. They did so by acquiring skills with the very weapons the Hyksos had introduced to Egypt.

With the coming of the Eighteenth Dynasty, Egypt entered a phase of empire building. This period was known as the New Kingdom. During the war with the Hyksos, which lasted almost half a century, the Egyptians learned how to become warriors.

Under Amenhotep I, the country became united again and was launched on a period of prosperity that was to last for 150 years.

It was during this Eighteenth Dynasty that an unusual event occurred. When a pharaoh named Thutmose II died, the throne should have gone to his son Thutmose III. Since the latter was a small child, the queen was appointed ruler temporarily — supposedly only until Thutmose III was old enough to reign. But the queen, Hatshepsut, was a woman of great strength and determination. For twenty years, until the time of her death, she ruled Egypt, wearing the double crown of both Upper and Lower Egypt, with all the power of a pharaoh. She was the first woman in Egyptian history to fill this role and was considered by the people to have all the powers of a deity. She kept Egypt solidly united and built a number of great monuments.

Hatshepsut made one major mistake during her reign, which was a prosperous one and remarkable in many ways.

She so dominated Thutmose III, who was the legitimate heir to the throne, that she incurred his lasting hatred. When she died, Thutmose III removed her name from all of the temples on which it had been inscribed. Despite this, Hatshepsut lives in history as one of the greatest women of all times and a powerful leader.

Thutmose III also went on to become one of Egypt's greatest pharaohs. He was a military strategist who built the nation into a world power. He planned some seventeen successive campaigns in Asia, leading them as Egypt's general as well as king. He turned a skeleton army into a powerful military machine that depended heavily on its spearmen and archers. Most important, Thutmose III saw the value of the two-wheeled chariots that the Hyksos had once used to invade Egypt. He had his engineers design a lighter, more maneuverable model. It proved to be the army's most

*Amenhotep IV (far left) married Queen Nefertiti (left). This queen is considered to be perhaps the most beautiful woman in history.*

effective weapon as the drivers and their accompanying archers attacked enemy forces far from the boundaries of Egypt.

By the time the reign of Thutmose III ended, after fifty-four years, the Egyptian empire had been extended into Libya, the Sudan, Palestine, Syria, and Mesopotamia. In addition, Egypt was receiving tribute from a number of other countries, including Crete, Arabia, and Babylonia. Thutmose III was such an excellent administrator that his successors were able easily to consolidate all these territorial gains. They then spent most of their time and efforts building new temples and public structures along the Nile.

One of the most interesting pharaohs of the New Kingdom was Amenhotep IV. He was not a great builder and certainly not a military leader. Rather he was a philosopher, so deeply interested in spiritual matters that he has sometimes been referred to as a religious fanatic. He challenged the priests of his day, ultimately forcing them to abandon their old gods and accept a new one, Aton, as the single, supreme being. He had an interesting philosophy that was actually quite scientific in its concept. Aton, he proclaimed, could be found everywhere because his presence radiated heat. Thus he could be said to inhabit the bodies of human beings and animals and plants. His rays were all-powerful and present everywhere. In a land like Egypt, this idea was easy to accept. Where could a person fail to find evidence of rays of heat?

As further example of his faith, Amenhotep IV changed his name to Akhenaton, which means "faithful to Aton." He moved his capital to a site some 200 miles (322 kilometers) south of present-day Cairo and called it Akhenaton.

## THE EVER-CHANGING CYCLES

The history of ancient Egypt is like a series of ocean waves, rising and falling in succession. Akhenaton's reign generated many fine works of art that have been unearthed by archaeologists, including some remarkable paintings that show scenes of animals, birds, flowers, and people in lifelike fashion. But the pharaoh failed as a ruler. His country did not emerge strong and prosperous at the end of his reign. The priests who had been forced to change their religious beliefs did so reluctantly. In no time at all they went back to the worship of many old gods and abandoned the faith in Aton. Furthermore, since Akhenaton paid little attention to those foreign lands conquered by his predecessors, Egypt's enemies quickly reclaimed what had been taken from them. By the year 1342 B.C. when the Nineteeth Dynasty began, Egypt's fortunes again were on the decline.

There was a short period, however, when the country had moments of glory, chiefly under Ramses II. He was ambitious and determined to win back some of the lost lands. With this in mind, he led an army of four divisions—some twenty thousand soldiers—against the Hittites who then were in control of Syria. He attacked the key city of Kadesh on the Orontes River, at the end of a wide valley. But he was too impatient.

He rashly led a single division against the Hittites, believing them to be much weaker than they actually were. As as result, he

*The temple of Ramses II at Abu Simbel*

lost many brave men and almost lost his own life. Yet he continued to charge, with only a handful of elite soldiers of his own bodyguard. This so diverted the Hittites that they faltered just long enough for the Egyptians to regroup and avoid a devastating retreat.

What has been called "the greatest battle of ancient times" ended in neither victory nor defeat. The Hittites retreated into the walled city of Kadesh, and the Egyptians were unable to complete the conquest they had hoped for. Ramses II tried to claim victory by inscribing the story of his campaign in glowing terms on the walls of many temples. But his greatest accomplishment was actually the negotiation of a peace treaty some years later. It kept the two nations on friendly terms for many years, neither one ever holding any great balance of power.

By the time Ramses III came to power in the Twentieth Dynasty, Egypt was under regular attack. Ramses III constantly had to be on the alert against invasion from the Mediterranean, too. The Greeks and the Philistines were among the sea people who looked upon Egypt as a possible prize. On one occasion, Ramses barely was able to prevent such an invasion when his ships held off an enemy force along the coast of Phoenicia. This was the first major naval battle in ancient history.

## THE DECLINE OF ANCIENT EGYPT

The era of the three Ramses left Egypt with some imposing architectural monuments and great works of art, as well as a few impressive military victories. But the arrival of the Twenty-first Dynasty found the country split once more into Upper and Lower Egypt and racked by internal troubles. Most of the land that

*Portraits of Psamtik — also spelled Psammetich — (right) and Ramses II and Queen Nefrari (left)*

Egyptian troops had taken to the south many years earlier already had been lost. Two cities vied for recognition as the country's capital. The priests defied the authority of the king, sometimes through secret intrigues, but many times in open rebellion.

In the year 945 B.C., a man named Sheshonk grew powerful. He seized control of both Upper and Lower Egypt and established a new dynasty (the Twenty-second). Sheshonk was not a member of the royal family, but a Libyan who had lived in Heracleopolis and came from a family of high priests. For a time he held control and even gained enough followers to raid a number of cities in Palestine and Jerusalem. The resulting plunder brought a certain amount of prosperity to Egypt.

The downfall of this dynasty came when a group from Thebes, largely made up of priests, weakened the already shaky rulership of the king. The Nubians to the south, sensing Egypt's weakness, invaded. They held the country for seventy years. But they, too, found themselves overwhelmed by administrative problems and were driven out by the Assyrians, who invaded from the east.

This kind of seesawing history continued when a prince from the city of Sais convinced the Assyrians they would have more control if he were to establish a Council of Princes as a kind of advisory body. To their regret, the Assyrians agreed. In no time at all the prince had amassed a large body of supporters and announced that he was now king. Using the name of Psamtik I, he founded the Saite dynasty (actually the Twenty-sixth).

*Memnon colossi, built thousands of years ago, are eroding but fascinating examples of Egyptian art.*

Under Psamtik and the Saite kings who followed him, Egypt enjoyed almost 150 years of peace and some prosperity. But it was a hollow revival of ancient glory. Much of the trade was carried on by foreigners; the king depended on Greek soldiers, who were paid as mercenaries; and few Egyptians played any part in building a rather sizable Mediterranean commercial fleet. In short, the renaissance of the Egyptian spirit was largely artificial.

The end of the dynasty came in 525 B.C., when Egypt attracted the interest of the Persians, who had been forging a powerful empire under their emperor, Cyrus the Great. Cambyses, the son of Cyrus, easily overran the country with his troops. He was followed by Darius I and Darius II, as well as by a second Cambyses. Unfortunately, only the first ruler, Darius the Great, ever showed much interest in Egypt. The Persians seldom visited its great monuments of the past, and used the land and the skills of the Egyptian artisans and engineers largely to provide materials, products, and money to nourish the Persian Empire. In many cases, Egyptians were mistreated and looked down upon. Isolated revolts thus became commonplace during the 120 years of Persian rule, which is called (though without great meaning) the Twenty-seventh Dynasty.

Three more Egyptian dynasties are recorded. They cover a period of seventy-three years during which Egypt was able to maintain an unsatisfactory kind of independence. The Persians, though still in control, had grown disinterested. They went on to other conquests; besides, they had stripped Egypt of most of the wealth. During this era, the capital was moved from Sais to Mendes and then to Sebennytos, symbolizing the changing fortunes of the various administrations.

In the year 333 B.C. the famed Grecian hero Alexander the Great won an important victory over the Persian army led by Darius III. The battle did not take place in Egypt, but rather at Issus, an ancient coastal town near the river Pinarus. Nevertheless, the outcome directly affected Egypt's future. Alexander had long been interested in Egypt's culture and its remarkable history. He ousted the Persians and actually was welcomed by the Egyptian rulers and their people as a liberator. Their response was justified, for Alexander made wide-ranging plans to improve the country and rebuild its literature and art.

One of Alexander's initial achievements was to found the city of Alexandria at the fringe of the Nile Delta. It soon became a great commercial metropolis and, perhaps even more important, the intellectual center of the entire Mediterranean world.

Egypt was for the first time becoming a part of the Hellenistic world. It is interesting to note that Alexander the Great was equally influenced by the Egyptians. He personally accepted the belief in Egyptian gods and was revered by the high priests of the land. It is said that this great leader also asked Egyptian soothsayers for advice about military and public matters.

When Alexander died in 323 B.C., Egypt came under the rule of another Greek leader, who made himself king under the name of Ptolemy I. He was followed by many other Ptolemies. They ruled Egypt as Greeks and did not bother to learn the native language. The last of their line was a person who has become famous in literature as well as in history: Queen Cleopatra. She showed interest in Egyptian affairs, accepted much of the country's culture and way of life, and spoke the Egyptian language.

By the time of Cleopatra's reign, Greek rule was seriously threatened throughout Egypt. The Ptolemies quarreled among themselves and resorted to numerous acts of corruption. Their reign constantly was being challenged by Egyptian uprisings. Finally, as we know from the dramatic works of Shakespeare and George Bernard Shaw, the rule of the Ptolemies was so weakened that the Greeks had to rely on Roman legions to keep the country from uprising. It was during this unsteady period that Cleopatra met and fell in love with the Roman leaders Julius Caesar and Marc Antony. A proud and fickle queen, Cleopatra committed suicide with the bite of a poisonous snake. At that time, 30 B.C., the Greek rule of the Ptolemies ended.


## THE ROMAN, BYZANTINE, AND ARABIAN PERIODS

Egypt was under the domination of the Romans for about three hundred and fifty years, starting with one of the most famous of all Roman leaders, the Emperor Augustus. Although Augustus

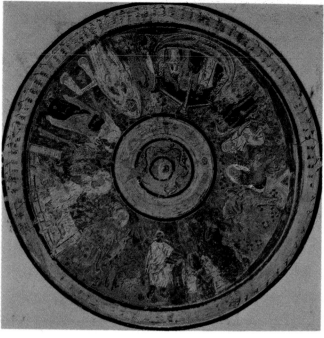

*Left: Portrait of a man painted on wood during the Roman period about A.D. 200*
*Above: Biblical scenes painted on the dome of a Coptic church at El Bagawat, Khargy Oasis (Kharijah Oasis)*

took the title of pharaoh, he spent most of his time in Rome. A great statesman and administrator, he simply did not have time to attend to the affairs of a foreign land. During the Roman period, Egypt was governed by Roman officials called prefects. These men were intent on exploiting Egypt's vast fields of grain.

Egypt entered the Byzantine period three-and-a-half centuries after Augustus first took over. For the first time, Christianity became influential—an interesting development in an ancient land that always had been dominated by a variety of sun gods. Christianity is said to have been brought to Egypt by St. Mark. Its influence grew rapidly, in spite of the savage persecution of its believers. Alexandria was the center of the Christian faith in Egypt. The idea of monasticism began there and the figure of the Christian monk became a familiar sight on the streets of the city.

At this time Egypt was ruled by Christian emperors. One of them, Theodosius I, who reigned from A.D. 379 to 395, declared that Christianity was the official faith of the empire. He ordered the old Egyptian temples closed, but he was unable to suppress the belief of many Egyptians in the gods of their ancestors. The Coptic church, which still flourishes today, was the original center of Christianity during this Byzantine period.

Egypt was a weak country at this time, partly because of the religious differences, but largely because it again was split into many parts. The government tended to be feudal; that is, it reverted to a system whereby the people were grouped into small communities dominated by lords. These lords were all-powerful and looked upon the people of their domain as vassals or, at best, tenants. Some of the lords were cruel, holding their subjects in virtual slavery. Yet even the most lenient ones imposed heavy taxes and forced the people to work long hours. Egypt, thus disunited, was again a likely target for invasion.

This time, the invasion came from the east. In A.D. 639 a Muslim general, Amribn al-As, led a small army (possibly not more than five thousand camel troops) across the frontier from Syria. Resistance was weak, largely because the Egyptian people had little sympathy for their own rulers. Within three years the government of Egypt had passed into Arabian hands, mainly those of the military. The capital was moved from Alexandria to Al-Fustat ("The Camp"), a kind of temporary garrison located near what is now the site of Cairo.

The Arabians allowed the Coptic religion. Yet the Egyptians for the most part accepted the faith and culture of their new rulers. Within a short time, Arabic was replacing Greek and Coptic as the language of Egypt.

For more than three centuries Egypt was governed by rulers appointed by the caliphs (the governmental and spiritual rulers of Islam). At first, these governors were Arabs, but after the middle of the ninth century A.D., they were Turks. In A.D. 969, Egypt was invaded by Shiite Muslims from North Africa. The Shiite Muslims, known as the Fatimids, were religious rebels who opposed the old-line caliphs. They established a new capital called El-Qahira ("Cairo" in English), which meant "the victorious city." They also built a large mosque, Al-Azhar, as a center for culture and information. This was later to become the world's first university of Moslem learning.

The early Fatimid period brought considerable wealth to Egypt. For a time, Cairo was the heart of a vast empire that covered not only Egypt, but also southern Syria, much of North Africa, and part of the Arabian peninsula. Egyptian trading ships sailed the Mediterranean, the Red Sea, and the Indian Ocean. For the first time in centuries, Egyptian architecture, art, and culture flourished. Examples of the jewelry, pottery, metalwork, and glassware produced during this rule have survived to the present day.

By the eleventh century, the Fatimid governors had become mere figureheads under military command, powerless to control even their own ministers. In A.D. 1171, they were overthrown by a general named Saladin, who had been appointed by the Muslim ruler in Syria to preserve military power in Egypt. Saladin rose quickly to the top, proclaiming himself sultan of both Syria and Egypt. He ruled Egypt for a little more than twenty years, though much of his time and efforts were spent fighting the Crusaders and suppressing a number of civil wars.

For the next three centuries, Egypt was ruled by a strange

*Saladin, the great Muslim leader, fought the Crusaders. He took Jerusalem from the Christian Crusaders in 1187.*

group of people called the Mamelukes. Their rise to power was unexpected and unusual, for they had previously been slaves from Turkey and eastern Europe, with no history as rulers and leaders. From the lowly ranks of slaves they became mercenaries or hired soldiers. In time many of them advanced to positions of military advisers and counselors. Once they were in positions of importance and, in some cases, power, they secretly formed a Mameluke military unit. Seizing their opportunity, they overthrew the Ayyubid leaders, the descendants of Saladin, and made one of their own officers sultan.

Despite their uncultured background the Mamelukes did encourage the arts. They built superb mosques, particularly in Cairo. The Mamelukes also successfully defended both Syria and Egypt against Mongolian armies that were ravaging other countries nearby.

## OTTOMAN EGYPT: THE ARRIVAL OF THE TURKS

In many ways, it was astonishing that the Mamelukes were able to rule Egypt for so many centuries. They quarreled among each other. Rival groups were plotting constantly against the throne. As a result, it was rare that any Mameluke ruler was able to stay in power for as long as a decade. Yet they continued to rule until 1517, when an Ottoman sultan attacked and invaded the Mameluke empire on numerous fronts. He was Selim the First, sometimes referred to as Selim the Grim.

These Ottoman invaders were Turks. Though they were Muslims, they spoke a different language and came from a different culture. They stationed their troops in Cairo and other large centers and regularly sent money and goods back to their capital, Istanbul. During their reign of almost three centuries, the Turks did little to enrich the art and literature and architecture of Egypt. All they really cared about was exploiting what riches the country had to offer. Under this kind of domination, the Egyptians did their best to avoid learning the language of the Ottomans or acquiring the Turkish culture. They lived for the day when—as inevitably happened—the Ottoman power declined.

Freedom came from an unlikely quarter.

Almost without warning, Napoleon Bonaparte and his French troops arrived in 1798. They landed at Alexandria and marched south. They met little resistance from the Turks or the remaining Mamelukes, and were welcomed by most of the Egyptian people. Napoleon announced that his military action was to protect a number of French merchant companies that had complained of mistreatment. But his real intent was to establish a land route to India and take over much of the trading then controlled by France's great enemy, the British.

Napoleon's army was too thinly spread to exert power for long. Nevertheless, his brief invasion, which lasted only three years, performed a great service to Egypt. The Egyptians became the

*The discovery of the Rosetta Stone by a lieutenant in the French army of Napoleon led scholars to the key for interpreting the written records of the ancient Egyptians, such as these hierogylyphics.*

focus of considerable attention from the French, and later the British and other Europeans.

One significant spin-off of this French invasion was the discovery of the Rosetta Stone. In 1799 a French engineering officer, who was encamped near the Rosetta branch of the Nile River, noticed a curious looking block of stone buried in the mud. Thinking that the stone, of black basalt some 4 feet (1.2 meters) high and 2 feet (.61 meters) wide, was nothing more than a building block, he was about to pass by. But he was curious. After wiping off some of the mud, he saw it was a great tablet, containing inscriptions in three different forms: Greek, Egyptian hieroglyphics, and a later form of Egyptian writing.

This discovery turned out to be an official decree that dated back to 196 B.C., during the reign of King Ptolemy V. Called the "Rosetta Stone," it was quickly recognized by the French as a priceless artifact. French scholars were able eventually to translate the Egyptian messages, as well as the familiar Greek. For the first time it was realized that ancient hieroglyphics were a language that could be interpreted and understood. This was a milestone in Egyptian history. With the Rosetta Stone thousands upon thousands of writings inscribed on temple walls, on papyrus scrolls, and elsewhere could now be translated.

## THE OPENING OF EGYPT TO WESTERN CULTURE

After Napoleon was forced to withdraw his troops, the Ottomans edged back into power. They had never withdrawn completely, nor had all of the Mamelukes. In 1805, the Ottoman sultan appointed Mohammed Ali, an Albanian officer in the Turkish army, to become pasha (or ruler) of Egypt. Ali was in many ways a ruthless man. In 1811, after years of unsuccessful attempts to weaken the power of the Mamelukes, he invited about five hundred Mameluke officers to a banquet at his palace. After they had consumed too much food and wine, they were slaughtered by Ali's soldiers.

Now in full control of the country, Mohammed Ali started to modernize Egypt and to introduce Western civilization. He brought new strains of cotton from India, put specialists to work developing other crops, launched a building program, redistributed farmlands and dug new irrigation ditches. He introduced sugarcane into Egypt, built factories in the cities, and set up new methods of transportation.

For the first time, high-ranking Egyptians were encouraged to pursue studies in Europe that would help their country. Western scientists, agriculturists, and educators were invited to Egypt to lecture and in some cases supervise operations. The new pasha

*Mohammed Ali took over Egypt in 1807. An etching shows him forcing Egyptians into military service.*

also established military schools and began to train an Egyptian army, one that would be tightly controlled by his own officers. Not all of these efforts, however, were undertaken for the benefit of the Egyptian people. Mohammed Ali's burning ambition was to establish himself so securely in Egypt that even the Ottoman sultan would not be able to remove him or replace him with someone else.

In this he succeeded. When he died in 1849, the rulership remained in his family. But those who followed Mohammed Ali in his bloodline were far less ambitious and determined. The government became weaker. It became so indebted to European banks that its power and influence were seriously undermined. The only great accomplishment during this period was the building of the Suez Canal. Completed in 1869, it was hailed as one of the world's greatest wonders. Ironically, though, it was designed and built by a Frenchman (Ferdinand de Lesseps); brought death, injury, or poverty to thousands of peasants who were forced to labor along its route; and ended up as an economic disaster for Egypt. The British stepped in to bail out the Egyptian government and thus acquired more control over the canal than the Egyptians themselves had.

*Head of Tutankhamen of the Seventeenth Dynasty.*

As Egypt's economy slipped, her government weakened. A group of army officers revolted in 1879. This was an excuse for the British to interfere, which they did by bombarding Alexandria and defeating the Egyptian army commanded by Urabi in the Battle of Tall-al-Kabir in 1882. The outcome was a bitter blow to the Egyptians, who had hopes of overthrowing all of the outsiders.

The British started a form of occupation that was to last for forty years. Although this was a dismal period for the Egyptian self-government, they benefited in some ways from British rule. The economy was stimulated, largely through agricultural improvements that increased the yield of cotton and other crops. Transportation expanded and new shipping lanes opened. The port of Alexandria was modernized; the tourist trade was encouraged; and the Aswan Dam was built in 1902.

The study of Egyptology flourished. Archaeologists arrived from England to undertake careful and meticulous research into ancient history. This led to a number of significant discoveries, including that of the tomb of Tutankhamen.

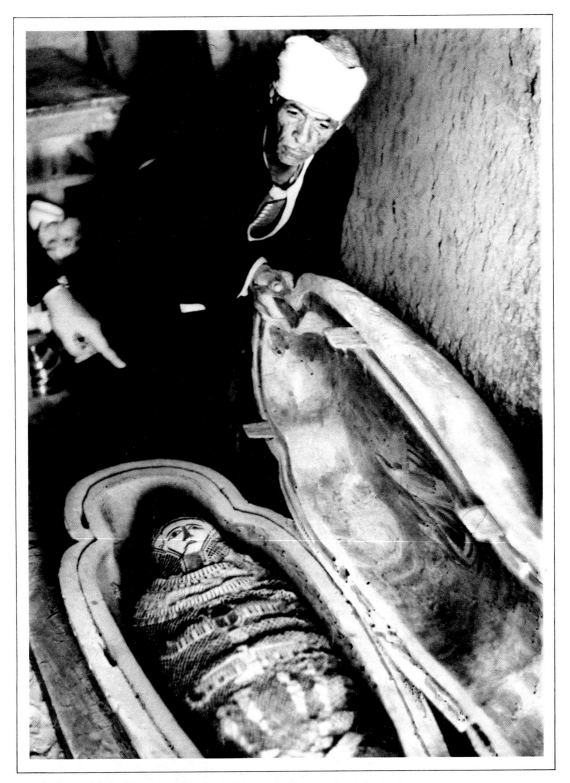

*Thousands of mummies were discovered in rock-hewn underground cemeteries not far from Sakkara.*

By the outbreak of World War I in 1914, the British considered Egypt little more than a colony. The war and the position of the nearby Turks as allies of the Germans gave the British excuses to tighten their hold on Egypt. But when the war ended, Great Britain faced revolts. The Egyptians began pressing for independence through an effective political group called Wafd ("delegation"), organized by Pasha Saad Zaghlul in 1918. After putting down a widespread revolt in 1919, led by Zaghlul, the British realized that change was needed. Consequently, they established the Kingdom of Egypt in 1922 and put King Fuad I on the throne.

The king was hardly more than a figurehead, yet his installation as ruler was a step in the right direction. Fuad was given little power. But he did establish the Egyptian University at Giza, the Arab Academy in Cairo, and a number of other institutions. Essentially, Egypt was considered independent, with its own constitution and parliament.

By this time, the Wafd movement had grown stronger. It was constantly at odds with Fuad and his successor, King Faruk, who ascended the throne in 1936 upon the death of his father. The British were forced to sign a treaty that promised Egypt more independence, as long as British troops could remain to protect the Suez Canal. Although the Wafd grudgingly accepted this treaty, it stepped up its anti-British campaign. It also fought the autocratic outlook of King Faruk and his lavish life-style.

During World War II, the relationship between Great Britain and Egypt remained the same. Egypt remained neutral for the most part, though Britain and the Allies retained bases within her territory. By 1946, dissenters were numerous, led not only by the Wafd but by extremist groups that violently opposed British interference and King Faruk's scandalous court.

*King Fuad I (left) was the father of King Faruk (right) who was deposed in 1952.*

Matters came to a head in 1948 when the independent state of Israel was formed in nearby Palestine, formerly a British mandate. The Egyptians, blaming the situation on the British, attacked the new nation. To everyone's astonishment, the Egyptian forces were beaten by a much smaller Israeli army.

About the only benefit the Egyptians salvaged directly was an armistice agreement that gave them administration of the Gaza Strip along the Sinai, largely populated by Arabs.

Indirectly, however, this defeat turned out to have certain blessings. It caused the country to unite, to review its objectives, and to achieve a new nationalism. The people were tired of the British and disgusted with the corruption of King Faruk. In July 1952, army officers, led by General Mohammed Naguib and Colonel Gamal Abdel Nasser, staged a bloodless revolution.

## INDEPENDENCE AT LAST

King Faruk had seen the revolt coming and fled to Italy. Few people realized it at the time, but it had been almost three

*Major General Mohammed Naguib (left) overthrew King Faruk and proclaimed Egypt a republic in 1953. Gamal Abdel Nasser (right), who had backed Naguib, took over and ruled Egypt from 1954 to 1970 when he died suddenly of a heart attack.*

thousand years since Egypt had enjoyed a purely Egyptian leadership. Mohammed Naguib, a highly respected military officer, headed the new government. He made it clear that the revolution, which had been so sudden that even the British had not had time to interfere, had two major goals. The first was to sever what controls the British still had—immediately and forever. The second was to break up the large feudal estates that were a burden to the people.

Egypt officially became a republic in 1953. A short time later Colonel Nasser was elected president and prime minister, replacing General Naguib. Nasser had been the prime mover of the 1952 coup, but since he was young and from a relatively humble background, he and his fellow officers had picked Naguib as the figurehead. Nasser was determined to improve the economy, effect social reforms, modernize industry, bring new technologies to agriculture, and pursue a more realistic foreign policy. A new era had begun, yet it was not without immense challenges for the country's leaders and the people.

In addition to the internal struggles to bring the nation into economic and political balance and undo all of the mistakes of the past, Egypt had to deal with exterior power struggles. These included relationship with Russia, changing presence of the British in many parts of the Middle East, and, of course, Egypt's position in regard to other Arab nations. Over a period of almost three decades, attempts were made to form a strong and lasting union with neighboring Arab states.

A major setback occurred in 1967. There was growing tension between Egypt and Israel.

Then in June of 1967, following stepped-up border skirmishes and military buildup, the Israeli army attacked with unexpected swiftness. By the end of what has been called the Six-Day War, Egypt had suffered a humiliating defeat. Israel had captured all of the territory of the United Arab Republic (Egypt's new name) east of the Suez Canal.

Although President Nasser offered to resign, he found that the country still was united behind him. The people felt that the outcome of the war was the result of forces beyond his control. He remained in office until he died of a heart attack in 1970. To Egypt's credit, the transfer of the presidency to Vice-President Anwar al Sadat went smoothly.

In 1971 the country's name was changed to the Arab Republic of Egypt. In 1973 President Sadat ordered a surprise attack across the Suez Canal. The Egyptian army was successful. The confidence and dignity of the army and people of Egypt were restored. Sadat became an international mediator, earning a reputation as a man of peace. He talked with his country's oldest and newest enemies to determine how to work together for a better future. His efforts did not prevent further conflicts with Israel, but they did succeed

When Anwar Sadat (left) was assassinated in 1981, Hosni Mubarak
(right) became the president of Egypt.

in effecting treaties and agreements that were positive and
forward-looking. It was ironic that Sadat, at the threshold of
peace-keeping achievements, was to become the victim of
assassins' bullets in October 1981.

The presidency was passed along with remarkable firmness to
his vice-president, Hosni Mubarak. Once again Egypt had
demonstrated the kind of strength that had weathered external
and internal storms for more than five thousand years.

In the 1980s, Egypt remains a nation of great, sometimes
incredible, contrasts. The country strives to establish democratic
principles, yet holds to customs and traditions that go back to the
days of the pharaohs. Egyptians continuously are seeking peace,
yet just as constantly are drawn into conflict. Enormous
technological and economic strides forward are offset by ever-
present problems of poverty and want. But the glorious past will
never fade, as long as a single pyramid is left standing and the
hieroglyphics on papyrus scrolls and stone tablets can be read.

This is Egypt—past, present, and future.

# Chapter 4

# *THE SPROUTING*
#           *CITIES AND TOWNS*

---

The birth and growth of cities and towns throughout Egypt have occurred sometimes in strange places and at unexpected periods in history. It has always been like that in the Land of the Sun. Caravans crossing a stretch of parched earth will come upon hidden springs and ridges sheltering them from the wind. The travelers will decide to form a camp in the desolate location. Eventually it will become a village, then a town, and perhaps someday a city.

Some cities were established in specific locations because certain pharaohs wanted them there. Perhaps a priest had proclaimed them holy places suitable for the construction of temples. Many villages sprang up because they were close to the river Nile, where the land was easier to irrigate, or where crops and livestock could be transported on barges. In any case, the pattern of civilization in Egypt began forming many centuries ago and has not changed much down through the ages. Most of the towns and cities hug the Nile or the delta region to the north. Others are situated on the Mediterranean Sea or the Gulf of Suez.

Yet there is a sprinkling of communities in the Western Desert. Why are they there? The oddest part about them is that most are permanent villages. They have existed for centuries and are likely to remain for centuries to come. Kharga, sometimes referred to as

Al Kharijah is one of these. It is an oasis in the south-central part of the country. Most of us think of an oasis as a tiny plot with a water hole, some clumps of palm trees and scraggly bushes, and a number of tents. But this is not a true picture. Kharijah, like many such desert settlements, is a village surrounded by irrigated fields producing vegetables, citrus fruits, dates, various cereals, and alfalfa. Populated chiefly by bedouins and Berbers, it lies along a railroad and carries on regular trade with other towns in Egypt. Its history goes back to ancient times, as is shown by the ruins of temples built by both the Persians and the Romans.

Several hundred miles directly north of Kharijah lies another desert civilization which probably had its origin as a tiny oasis or group of oases. It is Al Fayyum, situated in a vast basin in the Western Desert that is below sea level. It is irrigated by the Bahr Yusuf River, which connects to the Nile. Some of the canals originally were dug during the reign of King Amenemhet III earlier than 1800 B.C. The area is rich in cotton, fruits, and cereals, and apparently was an important agricultural settlement in prehistoric times. Many papyrus documents, written in Arabic as well as in Egyptian, have been unearthed in this region.

Today the city of Al Fayyum, a district capital, is an important industrial center of more than one hundred and fifty thousand people. As might be expected, it has factories that process cotton and produce fine fabrics. It also is active in the spinning of wool, weaving, dyeing, and tanning.

## FROM THE SMALLEST TO THE LARGEST

Egypt is a land of great contrasts. To see this in proper perspective, let's take an imaginary trip to two locations that are

*Irrigation at Al Fayyum (above) began more than three thousand
years ago. Crops, such as sugarcane (below), may be carried
to market by camel or truck.*

characteristically Egyptian, yet totally different in comparison with each other. The first trip will be to Bir Karawein, and the second to the nation's great capital, Cairo.

Bir Karawein lies in an oasis in the vast Western Desert and looks much the same as it did 100—or 1,000—years ago. The center of its existence is the village well, or *bir*, from which it gets the first part of its name. The well has sustained the people and the few crops and animals for generations. Without it, the village probably would die and be abandoned. There is, however, other water available. Oases are characteristically formed by subsurface water that seeps upward, as well as by open springs. Then, too, hills tend to cause more annual rainfall than in the flat regions of the desert. That is the case in this desert village.

A traveler would first see low and almost distorted hills in the distance. These hills appear to be without vegetation. But nearer to the base of the hills patches of green become visible, as do swaying date palms and then cultivated fields. The houses are small, built mainly of mud and rocks.

Early in the morning, most of the villagers are in the courtyard of the small mosque, praying to Allah before going out into the fields or to other places of work. The food preparation going on in homes, or the cooking or baking of bread, is kept private behind walls of clay and brick. In keeping with ancient customs, women are seldom seen in public and small children are not permitted to wander in the streets.

What kinds of businesses are conducted in the shops? There are people carding wool or weaving or sewing cotton into various items of clothing. Others work pieces of leather into sandals and belts and harnesses. A coppersmith makes vessels for holding water or food; an ironmonger pounds out nails and hooks; and a

In many villages the economic life and social customs have remained unchanged for centuries. But social programs and educational services are bringing about rapid changes.

*Markets (left) are called bazaars throughout Egypt. The handmade embroidered shoes (right) are an example of Egyptian handicrafts.*

carpenter fashions or repairs small items of furniture. There might even be a jeweler creating objects of gold or cutting semiprecious stones for ornamentation and ceremonial use.

In the center of the village numerous little carts are coming and going with various materials and wares—citrus fruits or onions and potatoes, raw wool, colored cloths, bundles of sticks, charcoal, tubs of precious topsoil, jugs of fresh water, bread and pastries, bales of straw, or sunbaked bricks. Some of the carts, particularly those with food, are pulled off to the side of the road, or in a public courtyard, where their owners proclaim wares for sale.

There are perhaps twelve thousand villages strewn across the Western Desert and the Eastern Desert, or hugging the hundreds of miles of Nile River banks from north to south, or pinpointing the rich lands of the Nile Delta and the shores of the Mediterranean. Many are like this tiny oasis village in character, in the daily activities, and in other ageless qualities that never seem to change. But others—and increasingly so—are much more modern, with houses of stone and brick, running water, electricity, large public buildings, and industrial plants. Cars and trucks are used more than the old-fashioned carts. Some even have a railroad terminal and long warehouses. But the little villages, depending on agriculture, still predominate and are likely to continue with few changes for hundreds of years to come.

Cairo has a life-style so different from that of the typical farming village that it would seem to lie at the opposite end of the earth. By Egyptian standards, Cairo is young, having been founded a mere 1,000 years ago. The name in Arabic, El-Qahira, means "victorious." The largest city in Africa and the Arab world, it has a population of about ten million. Cairo has been growing so fast that one of the capital's most challenging problems is trying to provide housing, transportation, and services for its people.

Like many of the oldest cities of the Western world, Cairo is a city of contrasts—ultramodern apartment buildings next to centuries-old mosques, narrow stone-paved alleyways abutting superhighways, the homes of the rich not far from the hovels of the poor. Glittering new stores display the latest fashions from Paris and New York. But a few minutes away in the bazaars of the Old Quarter, antiquated cubicles offer tapestries, exotic perfumes from Africa, strange confections, handwrought leather, and jewelry with designs dating back to the days of the pharaohs.

Cairo's skyline is punctured by the spires of hundreds of minarets (towers) of the Muslim mosques. Religion dominates

*Panoramic view of Cairo*

much of the life of the average Egyptian, just as it has for thousands of years. One of the oldest and most famous mosques is Ibn Tulun. It has the only spiral minaret in the world.

Two other features shape the character of Cairo. One, of course, is the Nile River. It runs through the western portion of the city and is alive with shipping much of the time. Just off the city lie two large islands, Gezira and Roda. These are largely residential and are considered suburbs. The second feature is the Citadel to the southeast. This landmark was built in the twelfth century by Saladin, when he was successfully defending the country against the Crusaders. The medieval section of the city is known as Grand Cairo. It lies in the shadow of the Citadel, evidence that the impressive walled city once was the heart of Cairo. Nearby is Al-Azhar, the oldest university still in operation. It was established 1,000 years ago as a center of Muslim theology. Today it includes modern science courses in its program.

Businessmen from America, Europe, the Middle East, and the Orient have investments in Cairo. Much of the money going into

*The massive Citadel built by Saladin*

A camel caravan (above) makes its way through the streets of Cairo.
Goods made of copper and brass (below) are sold at bazaars.

*An Egyptian (above) prays in a Cairo mosque. Children (left) learn to make and sell their crafts at this Cairo school. These items are sold to the thousands of tourists that flock to Egypt each year. This museum (right) holds many of the treasures of ancient Egypt.*

*Cairo traffic demands patience.*

new plants, oil exploration, agricultural development, real estate ventures, and scientific research comes from outside the borders of the nation.

Despite all this modernization, Cairo still strongly reflects its heritage. A slow-paced tide of daily life underlies the bustle. It is shown in the cheerful outlook of the Cairo inhabitants and their calm ability to cope with traffic delays and frustrations in placing telephone calls.

Ancient Egypt can be seen and heard throughout Cairo. Atop the minarets the chants of muezzins call the faithful to prayer. Tiny bazaars are jammed with copper vessels, gold and silver work, aromatic spices, inlaid chests, and carvings of ivory or ebony. On the river a low-hulled felucca with stained lateen sails barely edges its way upstream on the long route to ancient Thebes. Beyond the Citadel the Muqattam Hills stand as gaunt and rough-faced and desolate as they did in Predynastic times.

# THE SATELLITES

Egypt is becoming increasingly urbanized, despite its dependence upon agriculture. Realizing that Cairo would soon become a city of some eleven million people and that Alexandria, to the northwest, had three million people, the government developed a new plan several years ago. Its goal was to provide areas for business and industrial growth, yet not overtax the existing cities. Several satellite cities already have been established. The most important new cities are Sadat City, on the desert road to Alexandria and named after the late president; Nasr City, near Cairo; and Tenth of Ramadan City, near Ismailia and the Suez Canal.

These satellite cities are separate municipalities. They are not suburbs or extensions of the major cities near their borders. Sadat City, for example, has been designed to offer modern housing, convenient industrial sites, self-contained transportation networks, and all of the necessary services. The areas for these new communities eventually will total about 10,000 acres (4,047 hectares).

This was all part of a Five-Year Development Plan, which estimated that the economy would grow at the rate of about 10 percent each year during the mid-eighties and that the population would grow at the rate of some 3 percent during the same period. Space for living and working is at a premium in a country where more than 90 percent of the land is unpopulated and about 5 percent of the land must contain most of the population.

A list of the sprouting cities and towns would not be complete without mention of Alexandria, founded in 332 B.C. by Alexander the Great. The second largest city in Egypt, it is located on a strip

*Apartment buildings
in Alexandria*

of land between the Mediterranean Sea and Lake Mareotis, where it serves as a major port of the whole Mediterranean region. The ancient lighthouse on the peninsula of Pharos was considered to be one of the Seven Wonders of the Ancient World. Some 600 feet (183 meters) in height, the lighthouse stood for more than one thousand years before being destroyed by a devastating earthquake. Alexandria served as the capital of Egypt for about ten centuries. Today it is devoted to shipping and industry and is considered to be the "front door" to Egypt.

What lies ahead for the country's cities and towns?

Specialists in such matters foresee not only the birth and growth of satellite cities, but also a growth of communities along the northern reaches of the Nile, in the fertile delta region, and along the Gulf of Suez and the Sinai Peninsula to the east. An increase in shipping through the Suez Canal is one reason for this predicted growth. Another is that the Gulf of Suez holds great promise for offshore oil and the Sinai for onshore drilling.

*Tahrir Square, Cairo*

Yet despite this move toward the development of cities and the rise of industry, Egyptians will never forget the small towns and villages that for many generations have supported the people and the economy. For every plan aimed at city improvement, there are a dozen that focus on the future of the village. Such plans include land reform, agricultural development, new utilities, improved transportation, better housing, more schools, and more effective communications.

One official expressed it this way: "We see Egypt like a mighty wheel that we are all pushing forward. Cairo is the hub. But we cannot overlook the other communities—the spokes and the rim—for without them the wheel is useless."

Now a part of priceless museum collections, the gold diadem (above) was made during the Seventeenth or Eighteenth dynasty.
Below: The silver canister (left), the glass goblet (middle)
and the gold dish and beaker (right), made almost 3,500
years ago, show the variety of materials used by Egyptian artists.

Chapter 5

# SEEDS OF THE ECONOMY

The ancient Egyptians were blessed with two vital human traits. First, they were extremely industrious, working long hours from sunrise to sunset, day in and day out. Second, they were ingenious, applying their active imaginations to all aspects of daily life. These qualities helped to advance their early civilization far beyond those of other peoples in the Mediterranean region and elsewhere. Here are some of their achievements:

*Metalworking.* Thousands of years ago, the inhabitants of the region along the northern tip of the Red Sea discovered a mineral which today we call malachite. Dark green in color, it lay in chunks on the surface of the earth or just under it. It probably was first used in powdered form as a cosmetic, to heighten color of the cheekbones and enhance the eyes.

Later, some ancient artisan discovered that the green chunks could be melted to form that metal we know as copper. This led to the development of a small mining industry. Artifacts and excavations have indicated that some of these mines were so deep that the ore had to be hauled to the surface in baskets. The Egyptians perfected the art of smelting, or creating temperatures in excess of 1,832°F. (1,000° Celsius) so that the copper could be

*Temple of
Queen Nefertiti*

properly shaped and hardened. They learned how to mix the ore with charcoal, place it in a pit, and increase the temperature by fanning the coals with bellows. At first the ore was pounded into shape for instruments and decorative objects. Later, stone molds were developed so that castings could be made in quantity.

The Egyptians also were highly skilled in working with gold. They created masterpieces of jewelry admired down through the centuries. They also made useful objects from bronze and iron.

*Stonecutting.* The great pyramids, temples, and pillars prove that the Egyptians were probably the finest stonecutters in history. The earliest structures were made with sandstone or limestone. These materials can be cut and shaped quite easily because of their soft textures. Records show that metalsmiths made and hardened copper saws to cut limestone. But the stonecutters of the pharaohs were not dismayed when outcroppings of fine-grained granite were discovered and they were ordered to work this tough stone into building blocks. With great patience, they chipped away with instruments made of copper, iron, and stone itself.

They also used wood, in a way that demonstrates how imaginative the Egyptians could be. After cutting shallow grooves in immense chunks of granite or other stone, they would pound wooden wedges very tightly into these grooves. Then they would wet the wood, causing the fibers to expand. By using wedges and wetting them at the proper time, they could split gigantic faces of granite and crack them down to workable size.

Blocks of stone weighing 15 tons (13.6 metric tonnes) or more were moved great distances and raised to great heights. How was this done, without the use of cranes or other lifting devices? The stones were levered onto sledges, or sometimes barges, and towed to the desired location. There they were raised into place by being pulled up sloping earthen ramps. Once they were in position, the earth was simply scooped away and removed. The stones were dressed, or finished, with mallets made of diorite, a hard rock. Stone and metal chisels were used to cut flutings, figures, hieroglyphics, or other decorations on the surface.

Egyptian artists created small sculptures and jewelry from alabaster, lapis lazuli, carnelian, turquoise, quartz, and amethyst. Obsidian, a dark volcanic glass, also was used, especially for the eyes of statues.

*Pottery making.* Entire families specialized in this craft, largely because it required teamwork. The work was done most easily by groups living along a riverbank where the clay was of the right consistency. The smallest children could scoop the clay into baskets, having been trained to pick out stones and other undesirable elements. Older children then would carry the heavy baskets of clay, dangling from the ends of a pole, to a pottery shed, where it was kept moist. Lesser artisans would knead it patiently, sometimes mixing in carefully selected shreds of straw for added strength. After the clay had been properly tempered, the craftsmen would fashion dishes, pitchers, and other useful vessels on potter's wheels, which have changed very little in design and operation down through the years.

Although many clay objects were simply set out in the blazing sun to bake, others were fired in kilns. The kilns were made with domed tops to concentrate the heat, and had charcoal pits underneath. Some pottery, especially items made for persons of wealth, was decorated with colorful scenes before being fired.

*Weaving.* The Egyptians were masters at producing superb fabrics and weaving them into highly complex designs. Their linens were famous throughout the ancient world. Made from flax, a crop that flourishes in the Nile valley, they went through various stages of beating, carding, combing, and cutting into lengths suitable for spinning. Yet scientists cannot explain what mysterious processes made them resistant to aging. Some linens discovered in tombs were made thousands of years ago, yet are as strong as if they had been made in the twentieth century.

The Egyptians invented certain types of horizontal looms, then adapted them for vertical use. These machines were easy to use, accurate in operation, and capable of producing remarkably complex patterns. Although flax was the basic crop for producing fabrics in early times, cotton came into use later. It is now one of the most important manufacturing staples in Egypt.

*Papermaking.* Whether the Egyptians actually invented paper is not known. Yet it is certain that they produced one of the earliest forms of paper as we know it. It was undeniably finer, smoother, and more durable than any similar product of ancient times. They made it from an aquatic plant known as papyrus native to the marshes of the Nile valley and growing from 3 to 10 feet (.9 to 3

meters) in height. By pressing together thin strips of the pith of this plant, the early papermakers produced sheets that were white, fine-grained, and smooth.

The most important quality of papyrus was its durability. This has made it possible for archaeologists to interpret ancient records. Some papyrus did have the advantage of being preserved in dark recesses in completely dry air. Nevertheless, it is astonishing how well it has survived in comparison with Western records that go back only a few centuries.

*Lake Nasser was created by the construction of the High Dam south of Aswan.*

## AGRICULTURE: PILLAR OF EGYPT

Throughout history, Egypt has been dependent upon agriculture, and Egyptian agriculture has been dependent upon the Nile. That still is true today.

In the nineteenth century two revolutionary events occurred. The first was the development of canals, dams, irrigation ditches, and other works to assure a continuing water supply. The other was the introduction of cotton, which today has become the major crop and a major export.

The large Aswan Dam was started in 1898 and later was raised in height on two occasions. The High Dam south of Aswan was started in 1960. It holds an enormous water supply that makes up for those years when the floods from the mountains are small in scope. These dams have increased the amount of good farmland. They have made it possible for the Egyptians to rotate crops so they can produce two or three harvests each year instead of one.

It was Mohammed Ali who first saw that cotton could be a vital crop in Egypt. He brought in new strains of seeds from other countries, principally India. The rich soil along the Nile was ideal for growing cotton. Egypt exports some $400 million worth of cotton each year. Two other important crops are wheat and maize. The three crops occupy about 70 percent of all the cultivated land in Egypt.

Agriculture can no longer support the country as it once did. The main reason is that the increase in fertile land, though quite dramatic, has not kept pace with the increasing population. Yet there are indications this may change. Egypt cannot add much more land to the seven million acres (2,832,900 hectares) now under cultivation, but agricultural experts foresee ways to improve the productivity of the average acreage. Many of the farms are small and poor; they are irrigated and plowed as they have been for hundreds of years. As improved methods are applied, these acres will yield more produce. Equally important are new research projects destined to make the desert bloom.

One such method, recently developed in the American Southwest, is called drip irrigation. Plastic hoses, stretched alongside plants and punctured at intervals, drip mixtures of water, fertilizers, and pesticides. Experimental farms north of Cairo have been so successful that the per-acre yields of citrus fruits and grapes are almost as high as in the United States. Giant sprayers and sprinklers are fed with water and liquid fertilizers. They lay a fine mist over growing crops and have proved successful with corn, wheat, barley, oats, and other grains.

Equally exciting is a venture in the Nile Delta in which Egyptians and Americans have joined together to produce tomatoes on some 2,000 acres (809.4 hectares) of land. The soil is rich enough, when properly tended and fertilized, to produce half a billion tomatoes each year, many for export to Europe. One of the big advantages over similar tomato fields in the United States is that the Egyptian climate supports year-round growth, one crop after another, almost indefinitely. Since Egypt must import almost half of its food, agricultural experiments like this may one day help the country to be self-reliant.

Other crops that thrive in the Egyptian climate are rice, millet, onions, lentils, various oil seeds, dates, and potatoes. Sugarcane, a relatively new crop, is steadily spreading; sugar beets are being introduced; and citrus fruits look promising.

## THE GROWTH OF INDUSTRY

In the Eighteenth Dynasty of ancient Egypt, Queen Hatshepsut had visions of establishing international trade. It is recorded that in one early venture she dispatched a fleet of six long-oared ships down the Red Sea to the land of Punt (Somaliland). Her captains traded such products as knives, chisels, mallets, and weapons for exotic perfumes, myrrh, ivory, incense, and monkeys. Ever since, the Egyptians have taken advantage of their position as a cornerstone of Africa, the Middle East, and the Mediterranean to develop industry at home and carry on trade abroad.

Egypt never fostered the spirit of exploration across distant oceans as did the Greeks, Romans, and Phoenicians. Her shipbuilders designed craft for peaceful trading. They were heavy, with abundant storage capacity, and seaworthy enough to travel trade routes close to home. In a land where wood was a rare commodity, the builders showed great ingenuity by using reeds and sometimes the skins of animals.

Modern manufacturing in Egypt owes its origins to that same ruler who introduced cotton—Mohammed Ali. He imported machinery and hired foreign instructors so his people could learn the skills needed in the textile industry—using, of course, cotton. He was successful, but only partially so. Industrialization did not come to Egypt until well into the twentieth century. When it did, it brought an unexpected problem. Many people who acquired industrial skills in Egyptian factories began to seek jobs elsewhere. There they found more opportunities than they could hope for in their native land.

The problem still exists today, but there are signs that the tide is turning, as Egypt attracts foreign investments. American investment alone is more than $2 billion. Much of this is spent in salaries to train Egyptian workers, specialists, and the growing ranks of professionals. The overall plan is to turn raw materials into products and finished goods, and then sell them abroad. More jobs are developed internally and more profits earned if, for example, an Egyptian company sells finished clothing to a foreign distributor, instead of shipping out raw cotton to a nation where it will be made into clothing.

Among the industries developed in recent years are cotton spinning; weaving; cement manufacture; the processing of agricultural products such as tobacco, sugar, and cottonseed; and the production of petrochemicals, pharmaceuticals, and fertilizers. Because of the large-scale involvement in agriculture, Egypt places high priority on producing phosphates and nitrates for domestic use as fertilizers and is starting to export some of them.

Minerals and metals form another industrial base of growing importance to the economy. Copper, iron, and gold have played substantial parts in the country's development since ancient times.

Only recently, however, has Egypt tackled the challenge of producing pig iron, liquid steel, and related products. Much of the power for these growing industries comes from the country's two large hydroelectric plants at Aswan and Aswan High Dam, which provide about 60 percent of Egypt's electricity.

One of the brightest spots in Egypt's economic future may well be petroleum. The country started to explore for oil and gas in the 1930s and discovered a small oil field in 1938. Prospects are excellent in the Sinai Peninsula, the Gulf of Suez, and along certain sections of the Mediterranean coast. As a result, full-scale exploration is underway in these regions, where the government has joint working agreements with some thirty foreign oil companies. Egypt also has been constructing petroleum pipelines from the Gulf of Suez to the port of Alexandria. The highly efficient General Petroleum Company, run by Egyptians, exports about half of its output of some six hundred thousand barrels of oil per day. Major international oil companies, spending more than $500 million each year in exploration alone, include such names as Amoco, Conoco, Gulf, Mobil, and Shell.

The Suez Canal has had a multitude of problems since it was first opened in 1869. It has been staging a remarkable comeback since the reopening in 1975. Handling an average of more than sixty ships each day, the canal has tripled its business. In a long-range program that will be complete in the late 1980s, the canal will be widened and deepened, step by step, until it can accommodate about 90 percent of the world's supertankers. So, indirectly, Egypt stands to benefit economically from oil flowing outside its borders as well as inside.

Elsewhere in the country, transportation ranges from reasonably good to very poor. Unlike most nations with long

When the Suez Canal was reopened in 1975, teams of English, American, Egyptian, and French experts worked together to clear the canal of sunken ships and debris. The canal is a vital sea route.

histories and far-ranging borders, Egypt had almost no network of roads and highways until recently. Until the end of the nineteenth century, in fact, the main artery of transportation was the Nile. Only short roads were needed for local traffic to the Nile from nearby cities and villages. The caravans that crossed the open desert used camels. Consequently, the automobile made little impact on travel in Egypt until long after it was established as a means of transportation in America and Europe.

Today, highways are limited and poor, except in populated

Left: Tourists visit
the Great Pyramid at
Giza. Many have
their pictures taken
sitting on a camel.
Below: Khalili bazaar, Cairo

regions around large cities like Cairo, Alexandria, Suez, and Port Said. The existing network of roads encompasses some 20,000 miles (32,180 kilometers) in all, largely in the delta area and along the Red Sea coast.

Much of Egypt's internal movement of goods and materials is handled by a railway system that runs parallel to the Nile and the canals with a total of about 4,000 miles (6,436 kilometers) of track. Egypt was the first country in the Middle East to construct railways, with major links from Alexandria to Aswan, to the Libyan border, and to the Suez Canal. Although railroads today carry about 50 percent of all freight and some 30 percent of passenger traffic, the system is badly in need of overhaul and new equipment.

Egypt's economic story would be incomplete without mention of one more important industry—tourism. Each year tourists contribute over $700 million to the country. Generally, about eight hundred thousand tourists visit Egypt each year. Many come to explore historical and cultural wonders. Others are attracted by the sunny climate, scenic Nile, and beaches along the Mediterranean.

The economy of Egypt has some solid foundations, as well as great potential. Throughout its long history, Egypt has experienced just about every kind of governmental upheaval and internal crisis that can be imagined—and always has survived. Today, more than ever, Egypt is encouraging foreign capital and industry, and is moving away from a tightly controlled economy to that of an open market.

Such changes do not come quickly in a land that has been navigating its way through history for more than six thousand years. Yet eventually they will come and Egypt will continue to be a country of great appeal and wonder.

*The mummy of Ramses II, Ramses built the temples at Abu Simbel.*

# Chapter 6

# *CULTURAL*

# *ENHANCEMENTS*

---

In 1976, a most unusual Egyptian received an enthusiastic welcome in Paris, France, where crowds turned out to catch a glimpse of him. Those who expected to see his face were disappointed, and for good reason. He was Ramses II, who died in 1225 B.C. His mummified body was even more carefully wrapped than it had been when discovered in its tomb.

The mummy had been shipped from its showcase in Cairo's Egyptian Museum for treatment by French specialists. It was the first royal mummy ever to leave Egypt. A form of fungus somehow had invaded the airtight case and was threatening the preservation of Ramses II after more than three thousand years of mummification. Needless to say, the problem was solved and the ancient king was returned to Cairo.

This story illustrates the unusual nature of a civilization that intrigues the world today as it has for centuries in the past. Nowhere else on earth is there such an astonishing blend of history, art, customs, and beliefs as pervades Egyptian culture. The royal mummies are few indeed, yet they represent an enduring culture of death as well as life. Egypt's art included not only elements of beauty and imagination and creativity, but every facet of human experience.

*Tempera wall painting of an Egyptian queen playing a game found in the Valley of the Queens. Tomb paintings often showed scenes of daily life, such as hunting, sailing, or cooking.*

Painting and sculpture were elements of art. But so were religion, society, family relationships, clothing, transportation, food, common labor, health, recreation, communication, shelter, animal and plant life, and even common household effects. In Egypt a single art form or medium also represents history, religion, authority, society, and more.

*Wall paintings from the tomb of Nakht (Eighteenth Dynasty, about 1425 B.C.)*
*shows palace workers performing household tasks while Nakht and*
*his wife watch.*

Egyptian art is so traditional that it has changed very little in more than three thousand years. During the Old Kingdom era, groups of figures were painted standing on one line. Men, women, and children did not vary much in size or dress. Only rulers or other important personages were different, and invariably larger than the others. Birds and animals were commonplace in the art from this period. Many paintings, large and small, actually were elaborations of the hieroglyphic language. They told the story of life and death and birth, the nature of work, the administration of government, and the family in society.

*Statue of Menes in front of a museum*

Egyptologists—those who have studied Egypt closely and know much about its history and culture—are usually able to date works of art by style. They know that statues from the period of the Middle Kingdom (about 2050 to 1800 B.C.) are more formal and somewhat abstract. This has been called the "Memphite" tradition, influenced by the artisans of the city of Memphis. Statues of kings during this era wear stern expressions and have thick lips and high cheekbones.

Similar statues, paintings, or bas reliefs created at the end of the Middle Kingdom show a considerable change. That was the period when Egypt was dominated by the invading Hyksos. For many years the people were in contact with foreigners from Nubia to the south, Crete in the Mediterranean, and western Asia. These visitors influenced the culture of Egypt, particularly the art that has been preserved. For the first time, the formal and traditional expressions were infused with elements sometimes spiritual, sometimes emotional in nature.

This was a period when the arts flourished, possibly because it was a time of turmoil. The people who were creative were trying to understand life better by expressing themselves artistically. There was great variety in the art forms, evidences of experimentation, and a profusion of works. The immense building programs caused a need for more statues, more frescoes, more bas reliefs, more paintings than ever before. The sphinx—that imaginary creature with the body of a lion and the head of a human—was to become a kind of emblem for Egypt itself.

Many of the finest paintings that have been preserved came from the tombs at Thebes. These works, painted during the Eighteenth and Nineteenth Dynasties, have more flexibility and freedom than earlier paintings. Many are lively in format, and a few reveal a sense of humor, something not seen before in the art of ancient Egypt.

From the Twenty-second Dynasty through the Thirtieth, Egyptian art was beginning to show strong influences from outside, particularly Greek, but also Roman, Byzantine, and Arabian. The art of Egypt today shows many influences, most recently those of the Western nations. Yet many of the old traditions and ancient art forms persist. It is still true in much of the country's art, and in all aspects of its culture, that the works stand not so much as isolated forms but as integrated expressions of the many facets of life.

## THE EDUCATIONAL HERITAGE

A boy born in Egypt 150 years ago from a family above the peasant class would have gone to school. He would have been expected to arrive at the schoolhouse at a precise hour in the morning, with no freedom to express ideas or talk back to the teacher. Most of the subjects taught, however, would have concerned military matters and learning to be a good soldier.

The start of what might be called Western education came when that noted ruler Mohammed Ali decided that schools were important. He wanted young people to understand his viewpoints about the present and future of Egypt. Largely these were aimed at developing a strong Egyptian army. He wanted to make sure that he remained in office as supreme ruler and would not be recalled by the Ottoman sultans who had appointed him as ruling pasha.

Later in the century, around 1870, the government established a school system that was not based on military preparedness. It attempted to interest pupils in the history of the country and prepare them to help in improving Egypt. The schools were limited in number, however, and were attended by only a small proportion of the children in larger cities. Schools in small towns and rural areas were almost unheard of.

It was not until 1908 that a general university was founded, serving as an example for later colleges and universities in Egypt. The real beginnings of higher education date back to the early 1920s, when the country was given its so-called independent status by the British.

It might seem that the Egyptians have little regard for education, especially since the illiteracy rate today is above 50 percent. But that is misleading. Even in ancient times, the people were constantly being educated. However, the learning process was designed to accomplish two basic objectives.

The first was to establish the pharaoh or other ruler as a supreme being whose authority was not to be questioned. The second was to inform all people—whether members of the ruling

*Schoolchildren of Cairo*

class, middle-class merchants and traders, or peasants laboring in the fields or on building projects—about religious beliefs and responsibilities. In ancient times, such education concerned the power of the gods and the nature of the afterlife. With the coming of the Islamic religion, education culminated in the famous Al-Azhar University in Cairo, which has endured for more than one thousand years as the supreme school of theology in the Muslim world.

Today the whole educational system has been reorganized to provide equal educational opportunities and overcome the high rate of illiteracy. It is ironic that the school system should be so lagging in a country that pioneered in many fields of study. In ancient times, for instance, the Egyptians devised and perfected arithmetic, geometry, surveying, and engineering. Without these skills they never would have been able to plan and create the magnificent architectural wonders they left to posterity.

Later they recorded a mathematical system that was remarkably efficient and accurate. Their engineers and architects were familiar with geometrical progressions and could compute the areas of circles, ovals, and other shapes besides the square and the rectangle. They were far ahead of other civilizations in these matters. They also were capable of creating charts of the stars, celestial movements, and a calendar that is the direct prototype of the one we use today.

This kind of knowledge spilled over into other walks of life. The practice of medicine was well advanced during the later dynastic periods. When the Romans and the Greeks invaded Egypt, they often sent medical students to the Land of the Pharaohs to continue their studies. The medical heritage of Egypt, however, was spotty, probably because of the later influx of so many different cultures and customs and religious practices.

Modern Egypt compares favorably with other countries of the Middle East in its medical culture. However, life expectancy is low (fifty-four years) and infant mortality high (one out of ten births). The country is faced with many health problems. This situation stems largely from a shortage of doctors and nurses. There is a lack of health education in small towns and remote villages with only limited contact with the outside world.

## LITERATURE, MUSIC, THE DANCE

Egypt—and especially Cairo—has been called the cultural center of the Arab world. The publishing industry, while not large in comparison with that of some Western countries, distributes magazines and books to many foreign cities where Arabic is read. Egyptian poets, novelists, playwrights, and other writers are somewhat restricted by two powerful forces: the religious beliefs of Islam and political pressures. Yet there has been more freedom

*Seventeenth century copy of the Bible written in Arabic and Coptic script. This manuscript is decorated with colored illustrations and gold designs.*

in recent years so that they can express themselves without fear of censorship or suppression. Poetry is particularly vigorous, as the traditional form of literary expression in Arabian lands.

Some historians discount the immense accumulation of Egyptian writings as being factual records rather than literary works. But the Egyptians were the first people in history to develop a literary style and to nurture a true literary culture. Some scholars feel that the Bible itself owes some of its style and eloquence to the Egyptians. Others point to Egypt as the birthplace of the short story. We have examples from ancient times that include stories of adventure, travel, courage, and magic.

In certain of the old quarters in Cairo or Alexandria today, some of the finest artisans in the music world fashion flutes and small harps and other instruments. Egyptian music is a blend of the East and West, of many peoples and cultures.

Less is known about the music of ancient times than about other aspects of the country's life. Why should this be so, when there are such complete records of architecture and worship and rulers? Mainly because musical instruments were few and quite specialized; also, music was not written down on paper as it was in other civilizations.

We know that music played an important role in the courts of the pharaohs, in religious ceremonies, and probably in the day-to-day activities of the people. However, the music was largely vocal, and passed along from one generation to another without being written down. Many of the instruments were simple, such as rattles, clappers, and castinets. Others were makeshift drums, or flutes that were little more than reeds with holes punched in them.

Paintings from ancient times show few instruments recognizable today. Harmony was secondary; most of the action was geared to hand clapping, chanting, and movements of the hands and arms. Only rarely do paintings show a lute, flute, or lyre. Later, with the arrival of invaders from abroad, the Egyptians made use of such instruments as tambourines, harps, trumpets, oboes, and drums. Professional musicians, mainly singers and choirmasters, were highly honored in the courts.

Like music, dancing in the large cities of Egypt shows the influence of many cultures, Eastern and Western alike. Young people tend to prefer Western-style dancing. The traditional dancing preferred by those who preserve the older cultures is Arabic. The feet are not thrust out here and there to any great extent in rapid movements. Rather, they remain close together, almost undulating with the movement of the body.

Dancing in Egypt originally was associated with religious rituals, ceremonies, and mourning. It was a way to please the gods so that crops would be bountiful and the land fertile. Many dancers were professionals, supported and housed by the court. They took part in religious ceremonies, but they also performed for the pleasure of the pharaoh and his guests during banquets or on travels along the Nile on the royal barge.

*Wall painting in the tomb of Nakht found in the Valley of the Kings, Luxor*

Modern Egypt has been widely influenced by other civilizations in every facet of its culture—art, literature, music, education, and even architecture. Yet it is astonishing how much of the ancient culture has been preserved, how much of the old shines through the new. Few nations on earth, even those whose histories go back only a few hundred years, can claim this kind of miraculous preservation. And though Egypt is now committed to a program of taking its place in the world of tomorrow, one truth seems assured—it will never be separated entirely from its past.

# Chapter 7

# THE FACES
# OF A NATION

What image does the word *Egyptian* bring to mind? King Tut or Ramses? Queen Nefertiti or the ageless Cleopatra? Perhaps Cheops, the builder of the biggest Pyramids? Or the strong-minded Queen Hatshepsut? Or Thutmose III leading his spear-bearing troops into battle?

These are certainly Egyptians in the traditional meaning of the word. Yet all the ancient rulers of Egypt did not come from the same lineage. Cleopatra, for example, was a Ptolemy, a member of a family that originated in Macedonia, north of Greece. Other rulers had bloodlines that could be traced to Nubia, Assyria, Libya, and Persia. What then is a pure Egyptian?

The first Egyptians were classified as a race of people from North Africa known as Hammites, and were of Caucasian stock — that is, light skinned rather than dark. They were largely from the northeastern and Mediterranean divisions of this race. At the beginning of the First Dynasty, around 3000 B.C., and down through the end of the Twelfth Dynasty, in 1786 B.C., these Caucasian Hamitic origins probably remained almost intact. Then foreign invaders started to leave their mark on Egypt. They both influenced the culture and intermixed genetically.

Still later, some of the greatest leaders in history arrived, including Julius Caesar and the Romans, Alexander the Great and

*Jihan Sadat, wife of President Anwar Sadat, was a leader in working for legal rights of Egyptian women.*

the Greeks, Saladin and the Muslims, and Napoleon Bonaparte and the French. All of these nationalities influenced the faces of the people who comprise the nation of Egypt today.

The most populous nation in the Middle East, Egypt has some forty-five million people who are classed as native born or naturalized. Most of them live in the large cities of the north and along the Nile. Egypt is one of the few Arab countries where women are gaining equal legal status with men. The "Daughters of the Nile," as Egyptian women have become known, have been upgrading their status ever since one daring group demonstrated against the British more than sixty years ago by removing their traditional veils.

During the 1970s, Jihan Sadat helped to elevate women in the social structure. She appeared in public frequently (with her husband's approval), conducted numerous programs on behalf of women, and lobbied extensively on issues of concern to families. She launched educational programs to improve family solidarity and the rights of women in small, remote villages.

Traditionally, young girls of every class have had husbands selected for them by their families, often while the girls were still in their middle teens. Once married, they were "owned" by their husbands and were not permitted to come and go freely on their own. These conditions are changing in the modern, metropolitan areas. Girls are able to choose their own husbands, though preferably ones approved by their families.

Once it was considered unthinkable for a married woman with young children to go to work. Today more and more mothers hold jobs, usually leaving their children with older relatives. Single women are more likely to work. Because the family unit is very strong, single women live with their families until they marry.

This newfound status for women is not as revolutionary as it seems. In ancient times, women enjoyed exceptionally high and respected positions in Egyptian society. They did not wear veils, were not forced to live in seclusion, and were not excluded from activities that later became predominantly male oriented. Their rights were strictly protected. They could own real estate, inherit property, buy and sell goods, carry on trade and other business, and testify in court. They could even become pharaohs.

## PERSONAL APPEARANCES

What do Egyptians look like today? How do they resemble or differ from their ancestors of two and three thousand years ago?

The men, women, and children of Egypt, whether in a large city like Cairo, a town, or a village, consider themselves Arabs. That is

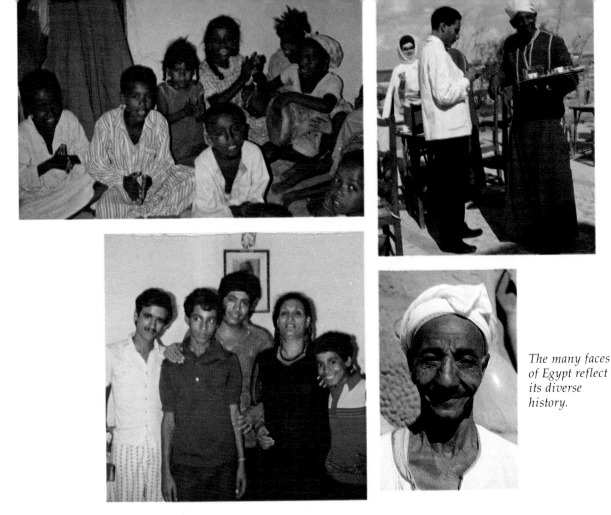

The many faces of Egypt reflect its diverse history.

reflected in the official name of the country—Arab Republic of Egypt. Their names will in all likelihood be Arabic, and will not bear any resemblance to those of the pharaohs or other noted persons in Egyptian history. Most of the people would be considered dark skinned, ranging from what looks like a perfect summer tan (northern Egypt) to tawny (central regions) to deep bronze or brown (southern). Some people from Upper Egypt areas are very dark skinned, the result of many generations of intermarriage with Nubians and other Africans. Egyptians take pride in claiming to make no distinctions for reasons of color. Yet it is true that many of Nubian stock, living in villages in southern Egypt, tend to stay together as families.

*A shoemaker works in this simple sidewalk shelter.*

Most Egyptians, men and women alike, wear Western-style suits and dresses in Cairo and the other large cities. In private homes or out in the small towns and rural areas, however, the clothing is more traditionally Egyptian, or Arabic. Men favor the comfortable loose-fitting *galabia*. Underneath its white folds they usually wear trousers of bleached cotton. As for headdress, some men prefer the skullcap, which is called a *libdeh*, while others favor the fez, usually red and in the ancient Turkish style.

Women in the villages or outlying areas often wear the hooded black robe called a *melaya*. This form of dress was traditional throughout Egypt, but now is worn mainly in the southern regions, where the climate is hot and oppressive.

## THE INNER LIFE

Little of the real life-style of the Egyptian personality (male or female) is evident to the foreigner.

Those who come to know the Egyptians are enchanted by their common traits. These include a fine sense of humor, the enjoyment of simple pleasures like singing and dancing, an innate commitment to hard work, and (oddly enough) a curious devotion to bureaucratic red tape and formality.

The Egyptian people are generally hospitable and congenial. Much of the hospitality and social intercourse is governed, though, by customs and traditions that foreign visitors should be careful to observe. A visitor to a family, for example, or to a businessman in his office or a teacher at a school, would probably be offered a cup of Turkish-style coffee, which is very dark, thick, and sweet. Or he might be handed a cup of hot tea flavored with mint or cinnamon. It is considered poor manners to refuse—almost like rejecting a gesture of friendship. It is much better to take a few sips, whatever one's reaction to the taste, than to explain politely that one does not drink coffee or tea.

On some occasions, Egyptian hosts and hostesses will pass around tiny sandwiches or little balls of a toastlike substance filled with pickled vegetables or tomatoes and lettuce. These are sometimes called street snacks, because they are sold by vendors on the city streets. People seem to be eating all the time, although in small quantities. Plentiful supplies of fruits are found in homes or sold in stalls along the streets. These include fresh dates, mangoes, figs, grapes, peaches, plums, bananas, and oranges.

At home young and old alike enjoy traditional Middle Eastern dishes. These include stuffed vegetables called *mahshi*; various types of kebabs not unlike the shish kebab Americans make on outdoor grills; ground mutton in a dish called *kofta*; *baklava*, a crisp, flaky pastry that is many-layered and oozing with syrup and ground nuts; and *semeet*, a pretzel-like bread.

The national dish is probably what the local chefs call *ful-medames*, dried beans that have been baked, flavored, and dressed with oil and lemon juice. This might be served with giant prawns from the Mediterranean coast, and followed by a popular sweet called *halvah*, made from crushed sesame seeds. Always, of course, there are various Arab breads and Turkish coffee or spiced hot tea.

*Pyramids at sunset*

Throughout Egypt, the family is the focal point of society, of religious belief, of emotional stability, of political outlook, and of continuing education. When young people leave the family circle, it is usually to find better jobs in other countries. Few sons and daughters ever leave home to live in their own apartments.

Over Egypt's long history, family life has been an important part of the culture for at least one significant reason: it was, and is, the seat of happiness. Even the peasants thousands of years ago (who were at one time mistakenly thought by historians to be little better than slaves) were encouraged to keep their family units intact. It was a time of joy when fathers and sons returned from the fields at dusk and enjoyed simple evening meals with their wives and daughters and sisters. Their huts of baked mud and straw were anything but elegant. Yet they never had to worry about the rain, extreme cold, and storms that have made life miserable for the poor in other parts of the world.

As social and cultural groups, the peasants of ancient times and the average citizens of today reflect an integrated concept of life. Religion, work, family relationships, and social outlooks all are bound together, cemented by deep traditions and customs. Pleasures tend to be simple: games, singing, dancing, and the observance of festival days. Until recently, the desire to travel abroad and to seek one's fortune outside of Egypt has not been strong. In fact, it is clear that foreign influences almost always have been generated by outside people coming into the country and not by the experiences of Egyptians invading other countries.

Egypt is changing and will continue to change. That is inevitable. But the evolution will be slow in coming. The people will remain much the same as today, and the ancient customs and traditions will continue. The Land of the Pharaohs is not likely to fade away until the great Pyramids crumble into dust.

## Cities and towns in Egypt

| | | | |
|---|---|---|---|
| Abū Sunbul (Abu Simbel) | D4 | Gazzāh (Gaza) | B4 |
| Akhmin | C4 | Gulf of Aqaba | C4 |
| Al Alamayn (El Alamein) | B3 | Halā'ib | D5 |
| Al 'Arish | B4 | Idfū | D4 |
| Al Bawiṭi | C3 | Ismā 'īlīyah | B4 |
| Alexandria (Al Iskandarīyah) | B3 | Isnā | C4 |
| Al Fayyūm | C4 | Jabal Kātrīnā | C4 |
| Al Ghurdaqah | C4 | Jirgā | C4 |
| Al Ismā Iliyah | B4 | Kalābishah | D4 |
| Al Jizah (Giza) | B4 | Kātrīnā Mountain | C4 |
| Al Khārijah | C4 | Kawm Umbū | D4 |
| Al Mansūrah | B4 | Khalīj-as Suways | C4 |
| Al Minyā | C4 | Khārijah (Al Wāhāt al) | C4 |
| Al Qusayr | CR | Lake Nasser | D4 |
| Al Uqsur (Luxor) | C4 | Libyan Plateau | B3 |
| Al Wāhāt ad Dākhilah | C3 | Luxor | C4 |
| Al Wāhāt al Bahriyah | C4 | Mallawī | C4 |
| Al Wāhāt al Farāfirah | C3 | Manfalūt | C4 |
| Al Wāhāt al Khārijah | C4 | Marsa Matrūh | B3 |
| Ash Shabb | D3 | Memphis (pyramids) | C4 |
| As Sallūm | B3 | Mūt | C3 |
| Aswān | D4 | Port Said | B4 |
| Aswān High Dam | D4 | Pyramids (Memphis) | C4 |
| Asyūt | C4 | Rosetta | B4 |
| Az Zaqāzīq | B4 | Qaṣr al Farāfirah | C3 |
| Bahriyah (Al Wāhāt-al) | C4 | Qattara Depression | C3 |
| Banhā | B4 | Qinā | C4 |
| Banī Suwayf | C4 | Quṣ | C4 |
| Bibā | C4 | Sawhāj | C4 |
| Birkat Qārūn | B4 | Sīdi Barrāni | B3 |
| Bi'r Misāhah | D3 | Sinai Peninsula | C4 |
| Būr Safājah (Safājah) | C4 | Siwah Oasis | C3 |
| Cairo | B4 | Suez Canal | B4 |
| Dākhilah (Al Wāhāt ad) | C3 | Tahṭā | C4 |
| Damanhūr | B4 | Tanṭā | B4 |
| Dayrūt | C4 | Thebes | C4 |
| Dishnā | C4 | Wādī al Allaqi | D5 |
| Dumyāt | B4 | Western Desert | C3 |
| Farā firah (Al Wāhāt al) | C3 | | |

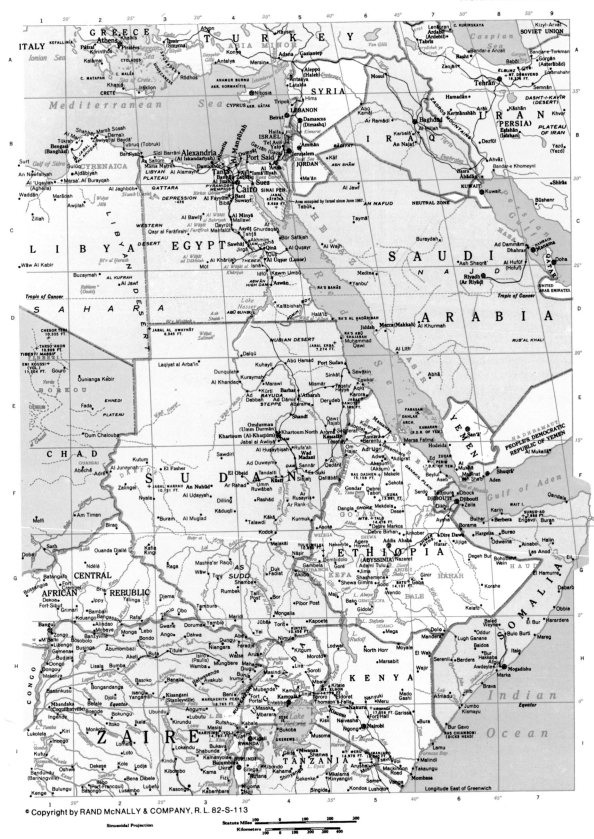

Sinusoidal Projection

Statute Miles

Kilometers

# MINIFACTS AT A GLANCE

## GENERAL INFORMATION

**Official Name:** Arab Republic of Egypt

**Capital:** Cairo. In Arabic the name is "El-Qahira," which means "victorious." Population: 6,133,000 (based on 1976 census)

**Official Language:** Arabic

**Government:** Egypt is a republic. Its constitution was adopted in 1971. The National Charter of 1962 states the goals of the republic. Only one person can run for president. The candidate is nominated by two thirds of the legislature and must be approved by a majority of voters. The president can serve any number of six-year terms. The president chooses a cabinet and one or more vice-presidents. The legislature, called the People's Assembly, has 360 members. They serve for five years. Voters elect 350 members and the president appoints 10 members. At least one half of the People's Assembly must be workers or farmers.

Egypt has twenty-five governorates or provinces, each of which is headed by a governor chosen by the president. All Egyptians over the age of eighteen must vote or they are fined.

**Flag:** The Egyptian flag has three wide stripes: red for sacrifice, white for purity, and black for the past. A golden hawk in the center of the flag stands for the tribe of Mohammed, the founder of Islam.

**National Song:** "Walla Zaman ya Silahi" (The Time Has Come To Reach for Our Arms)

**Religion:** Islam is the official religion. More than 90 percent of the people are Muslims. Less than 10 percent of the people are Christian Copts. Very few people are Roman Catholics, Jews, and Orthodox Greeks.

**Money:** Pounds, piasters, milliemes. There are 1,000 milliemes to the pound. There are 100 piasters to one pound. There are coins of 1, 2, 5, 10, and 20 piasters. Paper bills are issued in notes of 5, 10, 25, and 50 piasters and 1, 5, and 10 pounds.

**Weights and Measures:** Egypt uses the metric system. Egypt also uses some special units of measure. One rotl equals 4,449 grams (0.9905 lb.). One hundred artal (the plural of rotl) equals 1 kantar (99.05 lb.). One faddan or 333.3 kassabah equals 1.038 acres.

**Population:** 36,656,180, based on 1976 census. About 51 percent live in rural areas. About 49 percent live in cities. More than 90 percent of the land is unpopulated. About 99 percent live near the Nile or the Suez Canal. Estimated population growth: about 12.5 million more people by 1987. More people will live in urban areas.

Cities:

| | |
|---|---|
| Alexandria | 2,320,000 (official 1975 estimate) |
| Al Mahallah al Kubra | 271,373  ''   ''   '' |
| Aswan | 258,600  ''   ''   '' |
| Asyut | 202,700  ''   ''   '' |
| Az Zaqaziq | 200,800  ''   ''   '' |
| Cairo | 6,133,000 (official 1976 census) |
| Giza | 933,900  ''   ''   '' |
| Port Said | 349,000  ''   ''   '' |
| Suez | 381,000  ''   ''   '' |
| Tanta | 284,500  ''   ''   '' |

# GEOGRAPHY

**Highest Point:** Jabal Kātrina, 8, 668 feet (2,643 m)

**Lowest Point:** Qattara Depression, 436 feet (133 m) below sea level

**Rivers:** The Nile is the only river in Egypt. It has two branches: the Rosetta and Damietta rivers. The Nile River is 4,187 miles (6737 km) long. It flows through Egypt for more than 900 miles (1448 km).

**Lakes:** The largest lake in Egypt is man-made Lake Nasser, formed by the Aswan High Dam in 1971. Small natural lakes are Buheirat (this means "lake") Qarun, Maryut, el-Idku, el-Burulus, and el-Manzala.

**Deserts:** About 95 percent of Egypt is desert. The Sahara covers more than two thirds of Egypt. It consists of the Western or Libyan Desert and the Eastern or Arabian Desert. The Western Desert has uplands of over 3,000 feet (914 m) and depressions that fall below sea level.
The Eastern Desert has mountains of over 7,000 feet (2,134 m). The Sinai Peninsula is a desert, too. It has mountains of over 8,000 feet (2,438 m).
A small part of the Nubian Desert lies in Egypt. Only about 15 percent of the deserts have sand dunes.

**Oases:** Egypt has five important oases, all located in the Libyan Desert: Farafirah, Bahriyah, Dakhilah, Kharijah, and Siwah.

**Delta:** The Nile Delta is 100 miles (161 km) long and 155 miles (249 km) wide. It is shaped like a triangle.

**Climate:** The climate is hot and dry. There are only two seasons: winter (December through March) and summer (the rest of the year). Average temperature in winter: Between 55 and 70° F (13° C and 21° C). Average temperature in summer: Between 80 and 90° F (27° C and 32° C). In summer the temperature can be as high as 110° F (43° C).

**Average rainfall:** In Cairo the average annual rainfall is only 1 inch (25.4 mm). On the Mediterranean coast the average is 8 inches (203.2 mm).

**Area:** 386,662 square miles (1,001,454.5 sq. km)

**Distances:** East to West: 770 miles (1,238.93 km)
        North to South: 675 miles (1,086.08 km)

# NATURE

**Trees:** There are no forests in Egypt. There are date palm and citrus groves.

**Birds:** Egypt has about 300 types of birds.

**Animals:** Wild animals include the hyena, jackal, fox, wild boar, ibex, camel, and gazelle.

**Snakes:** The horned viper and hooded snake can be found in Egypt.

**Plants:** Papyrus grows between 3 (.9 m) and 9 feet (2.74 m) high along the Nile.

# EVERYDAY LIFE

**Homes:** In villages, peasants called fellahins live in houses of sun-dried mud bricks. These homes have one to three rooms. Bedouins live in tents in the desert.

**Food:** Egyptians do not eat much meat. They get protein from grains. Grain is made into a paste or baked into thin, flat loaves of bread.

This poor diet can cause diseases.

People eat small snacks, such as fruits (dates, mangoes, figs, grapes, peaches, apricots, plums, bananas, and oranges) or small balls of grain and vegetables. Adults drink Turkish-style coffee and hot cinnamon or mint tea.

**Holidays:** Unity Day—February 22
Revolution Day—July 23
Sham al-Nassim or Breath of Spring—a movable holiday following Eastern Orthodox Easter.
Movable Muslim religious holidays: Id al-Fitr and the Muslim New Year.

**What people do for a living:** 45% agriculture, 13% manufacturing and mining, 10% banking and trade, 5% construction, 4% transportation and communication, 1% housing, 1% utilities, 21% other services.

Business hours are from 9 A.M. to 1 P.M. and from 3:30 P.M. to 7 P.M. Friday is a day of rest.

**Culture:** The Egyptian Museum contains displays from prehistoric times to the sixth century. It was founded in 1900. There are many other museums in Egypt, including a post office museum, a railroad museum, a cotton museum, and religious museums. The largest library in Egypt, the Alexandria University Library, has over 1,000,000 books. Egypt has about forty different newspapers. There are over 1,000,000 radios and 200,000 television sets in Egypt.

**Health:** The life expectancy is 54 years. One out of ten babies die at birth. About 60 percent of the people have a disease called bilharziasis. There is a shortage of doctors and nurses.

**Customs:** Women earn less money than men even if they have the same jobs. Young women and young men live with their families until they marry.

The Islam religion allows a man to have four wives.

Fellahin families enjoy going to the village marketplace once a week to sell butter, chickens, eggs, and vegetables, and to watch street performers.

Bedouins move about the desert on camels and sleep in tents.

**Clothes:** In cities, men wear Western style suits. In rural areas men wear loose-fitting shirts called galabias and knee-length trousers made of cotton. To protect their heads from the sun they wear a skullcap called a libdeh or a fez. Women in rural areas wear a black hooded robe called a melaya. Both men and women wear heelless leather shoes or go barefoot. Bedouin men wrap cloths around their heads for protection. Most women wear veils that cover their faces.

**Transportation:** The Egyptian government owns the railroads. There are about 4,000 miles (6,436 km) of track. There are about 13,000 miles (2,0917 km) of roads. There are over 108,000 cars. People travel the desert on camels.

Egypt has nine airports. The largest is Cairo International Airport. Each year about 13,000 boats travel down the Nile River and Egypt's canals.

**Education:** About 75 percent of the people do not know how to read and write. Children between the ages of six and fifteen must attend school. But because there are not enough schools, only about 80 percent of elementary-school-age children and 20 percent of high-school-age children go to school. Government schools are free. Egypt has five state universities. The University of Al-Azhar in Cairo is one of the oldest universities in the world. It was opened in A.D. 970. About 145,000 people attend schools of higher learning.

**Chief Products:**

*Agricultural products:* Beans, clover, corn, cotton, millet, onions, potatoes, rice, sugarcane, wheat.

*Fishing:* sardines, shrimps.

*Manufacturing:* cement, chemicals, fertilizers, paper, processed foods, steel, textiles.

*Mining:* Gypsum, iron ore, manganese, petroleum phosphate rock, salt.

# EVERYDAY LIFE IN ANCIENT EGYPT

**Houses:** Ancient Egyptians lived in square or oblong houses built of mud or bricks made from mud. The houses opened onto courts. People slept on the roofs where it was cool.

**Food:** Ancient Egyptians ate grain, fish, and vegetables. Most people drank beer. On special occasions fruit, meat, and wine were served.

**Clothes:** Ancient Egyptian women wore long, tight dresses and bright cloaks. Men wore pleated skirts and capes. Both men and women wore black wigs to protect their heads from the sun.

**Recreation:** Ancient Egyptians played board games, and fished and hunted. Chariot racing also was popular. Children had pets. Girls played with dolls.

**Schools:** Girls did not go to school. Boys of wealthy parents attended school and learned to write and read.

# IMPORTANT DATES

| | | |
|---|---|---|
| 3100-2700 B.C. | Early Period | I-II Dynasties |
| 2700-2200 B.C. | Old Kingdom | III-VI Dynasties |
| 2200-2050 B.C. | First Intermediate Period | VII-XI Dynasties |
| 2050-1800 B.C. | Middle Kingdom | XII Dynasty |
| 1800-1570 B.C. | Second Intermediate Period | XIII-XVII Dynasties |
| 1570-1300 B.C. | Early New Kingdom | XVIII Dynasty |
| 1300-1090 B.C. | Later New Kingdom | XIX-XX Dynasties |
| 1090-945 B.C. | Post-Empire Period | XXI Dynasty |
| 945-730 B.C. | Libyan Period | XXII-XXIII Dynasties |
| 750-656 B.C. | Sudanese Period | XXIV-XXV Dynasties |
| 670-525 B.C. | Saite Period | XXVI Dynasty |
| 525-332 B.C. | Persian Period | XXVII-XXX Dynasties |

3100 B.C. — The Kingdom of Egypt formed by uniting Lower and Upper Egypt

3100 B.C. — City of Memphis founded

2500 B.C. — The worship of Ra becomes Egypt's first official religion

2100 B.C. — Thebes becomes the capital of Egypt

1900 B.C. — Egyptians may have dug a canal from the Nile Delta to the Red Sea

1700 B.C. — Hyksos conquer Egypt

1700 B.C. — Horses introduced by the Hyksos

1700 B.C. — Egyptians begin to travel by chariot

1570 B.C. — Hyksos driven out of Egypt

1370 B.C. — Amarna Revolution begins

525 B.C. — Persians drive the Assyrians out of Egypt and begin to rule the country

500 B.C. — Egyptians start to travel by camel

332 B.C. — Alexander the Great of Macedonia invades Egypt

332 B.C. — The city of Alexandria founded

300 B.C. — Egyptians first use coins

31 B.C. — Cleopatra's army defeated at the Battle of Actium

395 A.D. — Byzantine rule begins

639 — Arabic language brought to Egypt by Arabian invaders

642 — Muslim troops capture Alexandria

969 — Fatimids conquer Egypt

970 — The University of Al-Azhar founded

1171 — Saladin becomes sultan of Egypt

1187 — Saladin conquers Jerusalem

1250 — Mamelukes seize control of Egypt

1517 — Egypt falls under Turkish rule

1798 — Napoleon invades Egypt

1799 — Rosetta Stone discovered

1801 — French driven out of Egypt

1805 — Mohammed Ali becomes ruler of Egypt

1807 — British driven out of Alexandria

1811 — Mameluke leaders killed by Mohammed Ali

1820 — Long-staple cotton introduced in Egypt

1852 — The Egyptian Railways founded

1859 — Work on the Suez Canal begins

1869 — Suez Canal opens

1870 — First school system in Egypt is started

1875 — Egypt sells its share of the Suez Canal Company to Great Britain

1881 — Egyptians revolt against foreign control

1882 — Riots break out in Alexandria

1882 — Egypt taken over by the British government

1887 — Archaeologists discover the ruins of Amarna

1898 — National Bank of Egypt founded

1898 — Construction of the Aswan Dam begins

1902 — Aswan Dam completed

1914 — Egypt made a protectorate by Britain

1919 — Egyptians revolt against the British

1922 — Egypt becomes independent from Great Britain

1936 — Anglo-Egyptian Treaty signed; British troops leave Egypt, except for those guarding the Suez Canal

1938 — Oil fields discovered

1940 — Italy invades Egypt

1942 — Egyptian workers win the right to join trade unions

1942 — Germany driven out of Egypt by British forces

1945 — Egypt joins the United Nations

1948 — Egypt attacks Israel

1949 — Fighting between Egypt and Israel ends with the help of the United Nations

1950 — Egypt keeps ships from Israel out of the Suez Canal

1952 — Law limits the amount of land a person can own

1952 — King Faruk dethroned

1953 — Egypt becomes a republic

1953 — General Mohammed Naquib becomes the first president

1954 — General Nasser heads the government

1956 — Suez Canal nationalized

1956 — British troops forced to leave the Suez Canal bases

1956 — Israeli troops attack the Sinai Peninsula

1956 — Egyptian ships sunk to block the Suez Canal from European warships

1956 — Nasser elected president

1956 — Religious courts abolished

1956 — Egyptian constitution adopted

1958 — Egypt and Syria united as the United Arab Republic

1958 — Nasser becomes the president of the United Arab Republic

1959 — Arab Development Bank founded to help carry out economic projects

1959 — Suez Canal deepened and widened for larger ships

1960 — Construction begins on the Aswan High Dam

1960 — National health insurance started

1961 — Syria revolts and becomes independent from Egypt

1961 — All insurance companies nationalized; the Egyptian General Insurance Company founded

1962 — All banks in Egypt nationalized

1962 — Unemployment insurance begins

1962 — National Charter adopted

1962 — Egypt sends troops to help Yemen fight a civil war

1962 — Arab Socialist Union organized

1962 — The National Congress of Popular Forces meets; President Nasser presents the Charter for National Action to the congress

1964 — Egypt and Iraq agree to form a political union

1967 — Egypt and Israel fight a war for six days

1967 — Suez Canal blocked by sunken ships during the war with Israel

1968 — Aswan High Dam begins operating

1970 — Israel and Egypt agree to a cease-fire

1970 — Egypt, Libya, Sudan, and Syria agree to become a federation

1971 — Constitution adopted making Egypt a republic

1971 — Egypt's official name changed from United Arab Republic to Arab Republic of Egypt

1973 — Israel and Egypt at war for the fourth time

1975 — Israel agrees to remove troops from the Sinai Peninsula

1975 — Suez Canal reopened

1978 — U.S. President Jimmy Carter holds peace talks with the leaders of Israel and Egypt

1979 — Egypt forced to quit the Arab League

1979 — Israel and Egypt sign a peace treaty

# IMPORTANT PEOPLE

Alexander the Great (356-323), king of Macedonia, conquered Egypt and founded the city of Alexandria

Mohammed Ali (1769-1849), Viceroy of Egypt who killed Mamelukes

Amenemhet, the name of four kings of Egypt who ruled during the Twelfth Dynasty. Amenemhet I reigned from 2000-1970 B.C., II reigned from 1938-1903 B.C., III reigned from 1849-1801 B.C., IV reigned from 1801-1792 B.C.

Amenhotep I, king of Egypt who reigned from 1557-1540 B.C.

Amenhotep IV, king of Egypt who reigned from 1375-1358 B.C., began the worship of a single god, Aton. He changed his name to Akhenaton

Amribn al-As (594-664), Arab general who ruled Egypt from 642-644

Augustus (63 B.C.-A.D. 14), Roman ruler who defeated Cleopatra's army at the Battle of Actium

Cambyses II (529-522), Persian ruler who conquered Egypt

Cheops (dates unknown), king who erected Pyramids of Giza

Cleopatra (69-30 B.C.), queen of Egypt from 51-49 B.C. and 48-30 B.C.

Cyrus the Great (600-529), Persian king, father of Cambyses

Darius, name of three kings of Persia who conquered and ruled Egypt—Darius I or Darius the Great (558-486 B.C.), Darius II (birthdate unknown, died 404 B.C.), Darius III (birthdate unknown, died 330 B.C.), grandson of Darius II

Ferdinand de Lesseps (1805-1894), Frenchman who designed and built the Suez Canal

Faruk (1920-1965), king of Egypt from 1936 until he abdicated in 1952

Fatima (606-632), daughter of Mohammed, founder of the Fatimid dynasty

Fuad I (1868-1936), father of Faruk I, sultan of Egypt (1917-22), and king of Egypt (1922-1936)

Hatshepsut (dates unknown), queen during Eighteenth Dynasty, she preferred the arts and peace to war; daughter of Thutmose I, mother of Amenhotep II

Herodotus (born in fifth century B.C.), Greek historian who called Egypt "The Gift of the river"

Hyksos, the name of kings who reigned from 1650-1580 B.C., they brought horses to Egypt

Imhotep (dates unknown), member of King Zoser's court and builder of Pyramids

Menes (dates unknown), first king of Egypt, united Upper Egypt and Lower Egypt

Gamal Abdel Nasser (1918-1970), president of Egypt (1956-1958) and president of United Arab Republic (1958-1970)

Nefertiti (dates unknown), queen of Egypt during the fourteenth century B.C., wife of Akhenaton

Pepi II (dates unknown), king of Egypt for ninety years (2566-2476 B.C.)

Psamtik I (dates unknown), king of Egypt (663-609 B.C.), he fought against the Assyrians

Ptolemy I (367-283 B.C.), Greek who was king of Egypt (323-285 B.C.), he was a general in Alexander the Great's army

Ramses, the name of twelve kings of Egypt who ruled during the Nineteenth and Twentieth dynasties

Anwar al Sadat (1918-1981), president of Egypt from 1970 until he was killed by rebels in 1981

General Saladin (1138-1193), sultan of Egypt who conquered Syria and fought Crusaders

Selim I (Selim the Grim) (1467-1520), a Turkish sultan who invaded Egypt and fought the Mamelukes

Sesostris, the name of three kings of Egypt who ruled during the Twelfth Dynasty

Seti I (1313-1292 B.C.), son of Ramses I and father of Ramses II, fought Libyans and Syrians

Sheshonk (dates unknown), founder of the Twenty-second Dynasty, reigned from 945-924 B.C., he was Libyan and not a member of a royal family

Theodosius I (346-395), Roman leader who declared Christianity to be the official religion in Egypt

Thutmose, the name of four kings who ruled during the Eighteenth Dynasty. Thutmose II reigned jointly with his father. Thutmose III reigned jointly with Queen Hatshepsut, his half sister and wife

Tutankhamen, king of the Eighteenth Dynasty whose tomb was discovered in the Valley of the Kings

Pasha Saad Zaghlul (1860-1927), Egyptian lawyer who led a revolt against the British in 1919

Zoser (dates unknown), king of Egypt who decided to build monumental tombs, temples, and the Pyramids

# INDEX

**Page numbers that appear in boldface type indicate illustrations**

Abu Simbel, 34, 44, 94
acacia grove, **18**
Africa, 15, 16
afterworld, 13
agriculture, **12,** 58, 86-88
Akhenaton (Amenhotep IV), 42, **42,** 43, 124
Akhenaton (city), 43
Al-Azhar university, 52, 72, 101, 119, 121
Alexander the Great, 48, 49, 77, 120, 124
Alexandria, 8, 20, 48, 50, 51, 54, 58, 77, 78, **78,** 90, 93, 103, 117, 120, 121

Al Fayyum, 19, 66, **67**
Al-Fustat, 51
Ali, Mohammed, 56, 57, **57,** 87, 89, 100, 121, 124
Al Kharijah, 66
Al Mahallah al Kubra, 117
Amatrian culture, 25
Amenemhet I, 35, 124
Amenemhet II, 35, 124
Amenemhet III, 35, 66, 124
Amenemhet IV, 35, 124
Amenhotep I, 41, 124
Amenhotep III, 25
Amenhotep IV (Akhenaton), 42, **42,** 43, 124

Amon (god), 39, **39**
Amon-Ra (sun god), 11, 39
Amribn al-As, 51, 124
Amun of Thebes statue, **34**
animals, 118
Arab Academy, Cairo, 60
Arabia, 42
Arabian (Eastern) Desert, 18, 20, 70, 117
Arabian period, 51, 52, 99, 121
Arab Republic of Egypt, 63, 109, 116, 123
Arabs, 108
architecture, 30-32, 101
area, 117

art, 95-99
Assyrians, 46, 120
astronomy, 8-11, 34, 102
Asyut, 117
Aswan, 8, 16, 93, 117
Aswan Dam, 16, 22, 58, 86, 90, 121, 122
Aswan High Dam, 16, 22, 86, 90, 117, 123
Aton (god), 42, 43
Augustus (Roman emperor), 49, 50, 124
Ayyubid leaders, 53
Az Zaqaziq, 117
Babylonia, 42
Badari, 25
Badarian culture, 25
Bahriyah Oasis, 19, 117
Bahr Yusuf River, 66
bazaars, **4, 70,** 71, **74, 92**
bedouins, 66, 118, 119
bedouin tent, **9**
Berbers, 66
Bible manuscript, **103**
Biblical scenes, Coptic church, **50**
*bir* (well), 68
birds, 118
Bir Karawein, 68
Blue Nile, 13
*Book of the Dead, The,* **28**
bricks, 25
Buto, 26
Byzantine period, 50, 51, 99, 121
Caesar, Julius, 49
Cairo, **4,** 8, **9, 12,** 16, 20, 23, **23,** 51, 52, 53, 54, 60, 71, 72, **72-76,** 76, 77, **79, 92,** 93, 95, 101, 102, 103, 110, 116, 117, 119
calendar, ancient Egypt, 10, 11, 29, 102
caliphs, 52
Cambyses I, 47
Cambyses II, 47, 124
camel caravans **74,** 91
canals 13, 16, 20, 22, 57, 66, 86, 90, 93, 120
capital, 116
Caucasians, 106
chariots, horse-drawn, 40, 41, 120
Cheops, Great Pyramid, 32, **33,** 124
children, 68, **75,** 83, 99, 100, **101,** 119
Christianity, 50, 51
chronology, 120
Citadel, Cairo, 72, **73**
cities, 65-79
cities, major, 117

Cleopatra (Queen), 49, 121, 124
climate, 8, 18, 23, 117
clothes, 110, 119
communications, 118
constitution, 60, 118, 122, 123
copper, 25, 81, 89
Coptic church, 51
cotton, 56, 58, 84, 86, 87, 89, 121
Council of Princes, 46
crafts, 36, 70, 75
Crete, 35, 42, 98
crops, 16, 86-88, 119
Crusaders, 52
culture, 95-105, 118
Cyrus the Great, 47, 124
Dakhilah Oasis, 19, 68, 117
Damietta River, 17, 117
dams, 13, 16, 22, 58, 86, 90, 121, 122, 123
dancing, 104
Darius I (Darius the Great), 47, 124
Darius II, 47, 124
Darius III, 48, 124
dates, important, 120
"Daughters of the Nile," 107
de Lesseps, Ferdinand, 57, 124
delta, Nile River, **14** (map), 16, 17, 20, 26, 48, 71, 78, 87, 93, 117, 120
deserts, **6,** 8, 18, 19, 23, 26, **26,** 117
distances, greatest, 117
"Dog Star" (Sirius), 11
drip irrigation, 87
dynasties:
   First, 27, 106
   Third, 30, 31
   Fourth, 32
   Sixth, 30, 34
   Twelfth, 30, 35, 36, 37, 38, 106
   Thirteenth, 40
   Seventeenth, 37, 40, 58, 80
   Eighteenth, 40, 41, 80, 88, 97, 99
   Nineteenth, 43, 99
   Twentieth, 45
   Twenty-first, 45
   Twenty-second, 46, 99
   Twenty-sixth, 46
   Twenty-seventh, 48
   Thirtieth, 99
dynasties, dates of, 120
East Africa, 13
Eastern (Arabian) Desert, 18, 20, 70, 117
education, 52, 60, 72, 99-102, 119, 121
Egyptian Museum, Cairo, 95, 118

Egyptian University, Giza, 60
El Bagawat, Kharijah Oasis, 50
electricity, 90
El-Fustat ("The Camp"), 51
El-Qahira ("Cairo"), 52, 71, 116
ethnic groups, 106, 109
exports, 86-88, 90
Faiyum, 38
family life, 113
Farafirah Oasis, 19, 117
farming, **12,** 58, 86-88
Faruk (King), 60, 61, **61,** 120, 122, 124
Fatimids, 52, 121
fellahins, 118, 119
fez, 110, 119
First Intermediate Period, 34, 120
Five-Year Development Plan, 77
flag, 116
flax, 84
flooding of Nile River, 11, 13, 16, 39
food, 111, 118, 119
France, 54, 95, 121
Fuad I, 60, **61,** 124
*galabia,* 110, 119
Gaza Strip, 61
General Petroleum Company, 90
geography, 8, 15, 117
Gerzean Culture, 25
Gezira Island, 72
Giza (city), 60, 117
Giza, Great Pyramid, 10, **10, 92**
Giza pyramids, 32
gods, 7, 11, 13, 29, 34, 39, 42, 43, 49
government, 116
Grand Cairo, 72
Great Britain, 54, 57-62, 121, 122
Great Pyramid of Cheops, 32, **33**
Great Pyramid of Giza, 10, **10, 92**
Great Temple of Amon, Karnak, 11, **11,** 39
Greece, 35, 45, 48, 49, 99, 102
Gulf of Aqaba, 22
Gulf of Suez, 20, 22, 65, 78, 90
Hammites, 106
Hatshepsut (Queen), 41, 88, 124
health, 102, 118
Heracleopolis, 35, 46
Herodotus, 15, 26, 124
Hierakonpolis, 26
hieroglyphics, 28, 55, **55,** 56, 97
highest point, 117
hippopotamus figure, **36**
Hittites, 43, 45
holidays, 118
homes, 118, 119

"Horus on earth," 29
Horus statue, **29**
hospitality, 111
hydroelectricity, 90
Hyksos, 40, 98, 120, 124
Ibn Tulun mosque, 72
illiteracy rate, 100
Imhotep, 30, 31, 124
Indian Ocean, 52
industry, 88-90
irrigation, **12,**16, 22, **26,** 35, 86,
    87
Israel, 22, 61, 63, 64, 122, 123
Issus, 48
Istanbul, Turkey, 54
Jerusalem, 46, 53, 121
jewelry, 36, **37, 80**
Kadesh, Syria, 43, 45
Karnak temple, 11, **11,** 39
Khalili bazaar, Cairo, 4, **92**
khamsin wind, 23
Kharijah Oasis, 19, 66, 117
Khufu (see Cheops)
king, Lower Egypt, statue, **30**
Kingdom of Egypt (1922), 60
"Kingdom of the Two Lands,"
    27
Lake Mareotis, 78
Lake Nasser, 15, **86,** 117
lakes, 117
Land of the Sun, 13
languages, 51, 116, 121
laundry, women at village
    pump, **5**
*libdeh*, 110, 119
Libya, 42, 93, 123
Libyan Desert, 18, 117
lighthouse of Pharos, 78
literature, 102, 103
lords, feudal, 51
Lower Egypt, 26, 27, 30, 40, 41,
    45, 46, 120
lowest point, 18, 117
Luvironza River, 15
Luxor, 8, 105
malachite, 81
Mamelukes, 53, 54, 56, 121
manufacturing, 89, 119
maps of Egypt:
    Nile Delta, **14**
    political map, **115**
    topography, **2**
Marc Anthony, 49
marriage customs, 108
mastaba tombs, 30, 31
mathematics, 101
medicine, 102
Mediterranean Sea, 8, 15, 16, 20,
    38, 39, 52, 65, 78
*melaya*, 110, 119

Memnon colossi, **47**
Memphis, 27, 35, 98, 120
"Memphite" tradition of art, 98
Mendes, 48
Menes, 27, 124
Menes statue, **98**
Meryet-amun (Queen), 28
Mesopotamia, 42
metalworking, 81, 82
Middle Kingdom, 35, 40, 98, 120
monasticism, 50
money, 116
Mongolia, 53
mosques, 52, 53, 71, 72, **75**
mountains, 18, 117
Mubarak, Hosni, 64, **64**
mummies, **59, 94,** 95
mummifying, 28
Muqattam Hills, 76
museums, **75,** 95, 118
music, 103, 104
Muslims, 51, 52, 54, 101, 121
Naguib, Mohammed, 61, 62, **62**
Nakht, tomb wall paintings, **97,**
    **105**
Napoleon Bonaparte, 54, 56, 121
Naqada, 25
Nasr City, 77
Nasser, Gamal Abdel, 61-63, **62,**
    122, 124
Nefertari (Queen), 82
Nefertiti (Queen), **42,** 82, 124
Nefrari (Queen), **46**
Neolithic period, 24, 26
New Kingdom, 40, 120
Nile Delta, **14** (map), 16, 17, 20,
    26, 48, 71, 78, 87, 93, 117, 120
Nile River, 11, **12,** 13, 15-18, 24,
    26, 27, 39, 55, 65, 66, 70, 72,
    78, 86, 91, 117
Nile River, Second Cataract of
    the, 25
Nile valley, 23, 24, 84
nomads, **6,** 19
North Africa, 52, 106
Nubia, 38, 46, 98, 109
Nubian Desert, 18, 117
oases, 19, 66, 68, 117
occupations, 118
oil, 22, 78, 90, 122
Old Kingdom (Old Empire), 27,
    97, 120
Orontes River, Syria, 43
Ottomans, 54, 56, 57, 100
Palestine, 35, 40, 42, 46, 61
papermaking, 28, 84, 85
papyrus, 24, 28, **28,** 84, 85, 118
Paris, France, 95
parliament, 60
pasha (ruler), 56

people of Egypt, 106-113, **109**
people of Egypt, important, list
    of, 124, 125
People's Assembly, 116
Pepi II, 34, 124
Period of Troubles, 34
Persians, 47, 48, 120
petroleum (oil), 22, 78, 90, 122
pharaohs, 29, 34, 35, 100
Pharos lighthouse, 78
Philistines, 45
Phoenicia, 45
Pinarus River, 48
plants, 118
population figures, 71, 77, 116,
    117
Port Said, 8, 20, **21,** 93, 117
pottery, 25, **25, 36, 37,** 83, 84
Predynastic period, 25, 40
prefects, Roman, 50
priests, ancient Egypt, 8, 28, 42,
    43, 46, 49
products, chief, 119
Psamtik I, 46, **46,** 47, 124
Ptah of Memphis statue, **34**
Ptolemies, 49
Ptolemy I, 49, 125
Ptolemy V, 55
Punt, 35, 88
Pyramids, 10, **10,** 28, 30-32, **31,**
    **33,** 82, 83, **92, 112**
Qattara Depression, 18, **18,** 117
Rafah, 22
railroads, 93, 119, 121
rainfall, 23, 27, 117
Ramses II, 43, 45, **46, 94,** 95, 125
Ramses II statue, **34**
Ramses III, 45, 125
record keeping, 28, 29, 85
Red Kingdom, 27
Red Sea, 15, 20, 35, 38, 52, 81, 88,
    93, 120
Re-Harakhty of Heliopolis
    statue, **34**
religion, 11, 13, 29, 39, 42, 43,
    50, 51, 71, 101, 116
rivers, 17, 66, 117
roads, 91, 93, 119
Roda Island, 72
Roman art, **50**
romans, 49, 50, 99, 102
Rosetta River, 17, 55, 117
Rosetta Stone, 55, 56, 121
Russia, 63
Sadat, Anwar al, 63, 64, **64,** 107,
    125
Sadat, Jihan, 107, **107**
Sadat City, 77
Sahara Desert, 18, 117
St. Mark, 50

Sais, 46, 48
Saite dynasty (Twenty-sixth),
    46, 47, 120
Sakkara, 31, 59
Saladin, 52, **53,** 72, 121, 125
sand dunes, 18, 117
satellite cities, 77-79
scarab, **25**
schools, 99, 100, 119, 121
seasons, 8, 23, 117
Sebennytos, 48
Second Cataract of the Nile, 25
Second Intermediate Period, 40,
    120
Selim the First (Selim the Grim),
    54, 125
Sesostris I, 35, 125
Sesostris II, 35, 125
Sesostris III, 35, 38, **38,** 125
Seven Wonders of the Ancient
    World, 32, 78
Shakespeare, William, 49
Shaw, George Bernard, 49
Shepherd Kings, 40
Sheshonk, 46, 125
shipbuilding, 88
Shiite Muslims, 52
shoemaker, **110**
Sinai Peninsula, 22, 61, 78, 90,
    117, 122, 123
Sirius ("Dog Star"), 11
Siwah Oasis, 19, 117

Six-Day War (1967), 22, 63
snakes, 118
soil, 13, 16, 17
Somaliland, 35, 88
song, national, 116
sphinx, 99
statues, **29, 30, 34, 39,** 98, **98**
Step Pyramid, 31, **31**
Stone Age, 24, 26
stonecutting, 82, 83
Sudan, 15, 18, 42, 123
Suez (city), 93, 117
Suez Canal, 20, 22, 57, 60, 78, 90,
    **91,** 93, 121, 122, 123
sugarcane, 56, **67,** 88
sun, its influence on Egypt, 7, 13
sun god, 7, 11, 13
Syria, 35, 38, 42, 43, 51, 52, 53,
    122, 123
Taba, 22
Tahrir Square, Cairo, **79**
Tanta, 117
Tall-al-Kabir, Battle of, 58
temperatures, 8, 19, 23, 117
temple, Karnak, 11, **11,** 39
Temple of Queen Nefertari, **82**
Temple of Ramses II, **44**
Tenth of Ramadan City, 77
Thebes, 38, 39, 46, 99, 120
Theodosius I, 51, 125
Thutmose II, 41, 125
Thutmose III, 41, 42, 125

tomatoes, 87-88
tomb paintings, **96, 97,** 99, **105**
tourism, 93
trade, 35, 38, 52, 88
transportation, 90-93, 119
trees, 118
Turkey, 53
Turks, 52, 54, 60, 121
Tutankhamen, 58, **58,** 125
United Arab Republic, 63, 122
universities, 52, 60, 72, 100, 119
Upper Egypt, 24, 25-26, 27, 40,
    41, 45, 46, 109, 120
Urabi, 58
Valley of the Kings, 37, 105
Valley of the Queens, 96
villages, **17,** 65, 66, 68, **69,** 70, 71,
    79
Wafd, 60
weaving, 84, **85**
weights and measures, 116
Western Desert, 18, 19, 65, 66,
    68, 70, 117
White Kingdom, 27
White Nile, 13
wind, 23
women, **5,** 41, 68, **68,** 107, 108,
    119
World War I, 60
World War II, 60
Zaghlul, Pasha Saad, 60, 125
Zoser (King), 30, 31, 125

## About the Author

Wilbur Cross, a professional writer and editor, is the author of some 20 non-fiction books and several hundred magazine articles. His subjects range widely from travel and foreign culture to history, sociology, medicine, business, adventure, biography, humor, education, and politics. In this book, he has touched on these and other subjects in the course of profiling the unique entity that is Egypt.

Mr. Cross served as a captain in the United States Army, with long service in the Pacific; worked for several years as a copywriter with a New York City advertising agency; and was an associate editor at *Life* magazine. He founded and directed his own firm, Books for Business, as an editorial director and consultant, and has worked as an editor and writer in the energy field.

Among his books are *Naval Battles and Heroes, Challengers of the Deep, Ghost Ship of the Pole, White House Weddings, Your Career in the Age of Automation, A Guide to Unusual Vacation, Kids and Booze,* and *Presidential Courage.*

Married and the father of four daughters, he lives in Westchester County, New York.